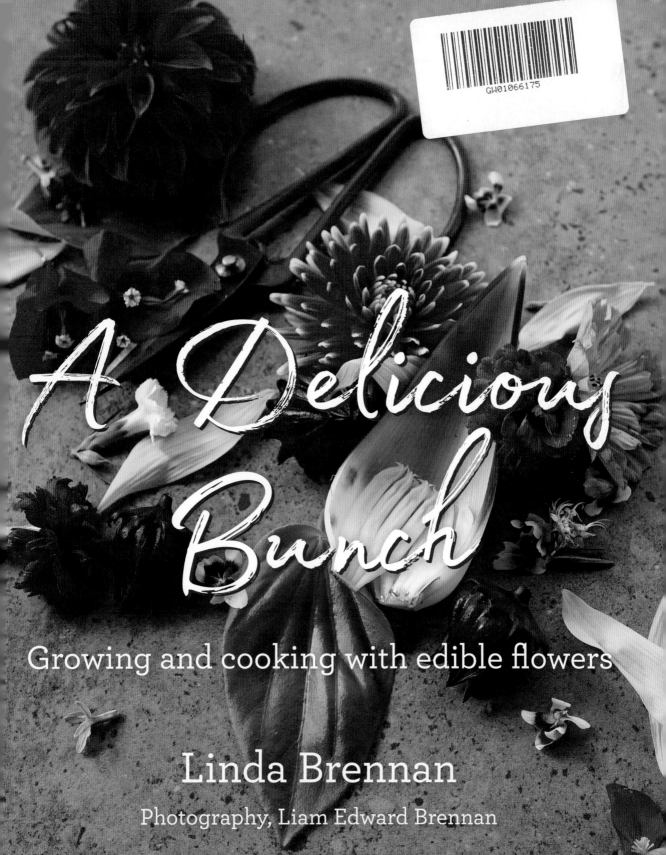

A Delicious Bunch

Growing and cooking with edible flowers

Linda Brennan

Photography, Liam Edward Brennan

Terms used in this book

ANNUAL: A plant that has a very short life, usually growing, flowering, setting seed and dying within a year. Sunflowers are an example of an annual plant.

PERENNIAL: A plant that lives for at least 2 years and is soft and herbaceous. Gingers and Society Garlic are examples of perennial plants. Some perennials such as Torch Ginger are deciduous, dying down in winter. Others such as Alyssum and Society Garlic remain evergreen.

FOLIAR FEED: Liquid fertiliser applied to the leaves usually via a sprayer. Foliar fertilisers are in a form that can be absorbed by the leaves.

PELLETISED FERTILISER: These organic fertilisers can be a combination of manures, seaweed and other natural ingredients.

STANDARD AUSTRALIAN
METRIC MEASURES ARE USED
THROUGHOUT
1 large egg = 59g
1 tablespoon = 20ml
1 dessertspoon = 15ml
1 teaspoon = 5ml
1 cup = 250 ml
g = grams
kg = kilograms
ml = millilitres

V= Vegetarian
GF = Gluten free
DF = Dairy free

CONTENTS

A delicious bunch

Have you seen flowers on or in your food and wondered whether or not you should eat them? This is the book for you. It shows you how to grow a beautiful, delicious bunch of edible flowers through the year.

I hope this book also tempts you to be adventurous in using flowers in your cooking. Blooming beautiful garnishes, fragrant perfumes and succulent meals made from flowers are enticing because of their colour, flavour and fragrance. They can create an expectation of enjoyment even before that first succulent mouthful.

A Delicious Bunch provides you with the essentials for growing and eating flowers in deliciously tempting ways. I have detailed 30 of my favourite flowers to share with you. We eat some almost daily, whereas others are strictly seasonal and we anticipate their blooming with eagerness each year. You will find a selection that can be grown across the country and that are well worth the space in your garden and on your plate.

For each beautiful bloom, there is a delicious recipe. Some, like the shortcake recipe, have been passed down from my mum who was a beautiful cook. Others, including the fabulous sour soup base for the Hummingbird Flower Soup, were generously shared by friends. The remainder are the result of my creative culinary endeavours over the years. My dedicated family of taste testers has had great fun assisting me!

I hope you are inspired to grow your own garden of edible flowers and enjoy the variety of ways that you can indulge your taste buds.

A blooming history

Edible flowers have brightened dinner plates through the ages. They have featured in forage baskets and vegetable gardens for generations of people across the world. The ancient Romans used mustard flowers as a love potion. In ancient Persia, the birthplace of roses, these gorgeous flowers were used medicinally and made into wine. We still have an enduring love affair with roses to this day.

A wide range of flowers flavour alcohol. Examples include hops for beer, violets in liqueurs and Clary Sage which is made into clary wine. A clary wine recipe appears in a family heirloom copy of Warne's Every Day Cookery Book, brought to Australia with my husband's grandmother when she arrived as a young woman. We wonder if she made the wine.

For many centuries, the Chinese have enjoyed day lilies, chrysanthemum, jasmine and calendula. In the Americas, indigenous peoples were eating yucca, nasturtiums, marigolds, clover and bee balm flowers. Across the oceans ancient Greeks made the most of saffron, poppies, carnations and fennel blossom. So, it's not just contemporary chefs in high end restaurants who have 'invented' floral cuisine. The use of flowers in food and drinks has a vast and rich history.

The use of edible flowers has grown in popularity more recently, with stunning punnets of pretty blossoms now in high demand. Some edible flowers are presented as a romantic garnish. Many such as daylilies, zucchini flowers and rosellas can be central to a dish. For example, I fill daylily flowers with a piped rosette of dairy-free sweet herbed 'cheese', or stir fry the buds as a savoury dish in the Japanese tradition. I make them by adding soy sauce and ginger in a little butter or oil and cooking quickly.

Do you sometimes wonder how you can possibly include edible flowers in your daily meals? Why not start with a morning herbal chai tea, complete with cornflowers or jasmine? You can enjoy breakfast granola infused with petals. Make a floral salad with all the benefits of antioxidants from the flowers. Your plain glass of water looks gorgeous dressed up with floral ice cubes. Serve your rose petal sorbet or Turkish delight ice-cream from a floral ice bowl – it is simply breathtaking. Dress a dish with a sprinkling of edible flowers in their colourful finery. Flowers can transform a plain dish into a spectacular, enticing and gloriously tempting delight.

Harvesting and storing edible flowers

Most of the flowers we eat are delicate and easily damaged. Aim to harvest your edible flowers as close to serving time as possible.

Here are some hot tips for storing your edible flowers for a day or two.

- Pick them early in the morning coolness, as soon as possible after the flowers have opened when they will be at their peak

- Use a little pair of flower scissors for accurate snipping. Collect blooms in a single layer in a shallow basket or bowl so they are not crushed. After collection, check for insects and discard any spoiled flowers. Cool your flowers or petals to 5°C as quickly as possible to preserve freshness. Pack into a lidded container and store in the fridge. Before use, check them for freshness

- Some flowers keep better and for longer than others. Violas and whole petite roses are terrific for 3-4 days. Edible ginger flowers keep 3-5 days in good condition without refrigeration, just sitting in a vase of fresh water. Jasmine tends to change colour quickly and won't keep well beyond the day of harvest. Daylilies and chicory flowers only last one day, so if you want them for a recipe you need to use the open flowers the same day

- To stockpile larger flowers over a few days, cut fresh, new buds with stems, put them straight into a vase of cool water and place them in a cool spot. The fridge is sometimes required on hot days. Sunflowers will close over when out of the light, so they need access to light unless you harvest and store the petals only

- If you have an abundance of flowers, try some of the preserving methods on pages 8-11.

Flowers in the kitchen

Some of our most common vegetables are actually flowers. Broccoli and cauliflower are perfect examples of immature flower heads. If you wait too long before harvest they can shoot long stems and grow heads of flowers almost to waist height. The little flowers are edible, making a delicious savoury addition to cheesy tartlets, salads and scrambled eggs.

COOKS LOVE FLOWERS

If you've travelled to Italy during spring and summer, you may remember the little trattorias serving up zucchini flowers. The blossoms are typically stuffed with fresh ricotta then deep-fried in a light batter until golden. This is one way to really enjoy these stunning flowers. I enjoyed zucchini flowers in little places all around the Cinque Terre on one memorable Italian holiday. It convinced me to make these ricotta-stuffed delights at home.

The French take the art of eating artichoke flowers to a delicious high. French recipes tempt you to enjoy the flower (thistle) bud with melted butter. Even better, in my opinion, is serving the cooked base (choke) with a blue cheese sauce.

Using the flowers of zucchini or any vegetables, means that you will forego fruit. This is not often an issue for something as prolific as zucchini or pumpkins. You'll be able to enjoy your plants at many stages of their life.

When I first began growing flowers to eat, my mind wandered to the European varieties: Roses, lavender, violets and borage. However, these English favourites can be a challenge to grow throughout warmer and more humid climatic regions. If you live in hotter regions, look at the floral food traditions that use heat-loving blooms—for example, Asia and Africa. I have included a number for you to trial in your warm garden, including the Blue Butterfly Vine, not to be confused with the Blue Butterfly Bush.

The Blue Butterfly Vine, *Clitoria ternatea*, makes a most wonderful natural blue colouring. This can be used in rice, custards or to colour cake icing. Asian cultures traditionally use it in celebratory dishes.

The Hummingbird Flower grows as an open pioneer species tree in the tropics and subtropics. It gives you quick open canopy for a narrow spot in your garden and provides you with leaves, pods and edible flowers, somewhat like the Moringa tree. Hummingbird flowers, also called Agati, are often used as a crisp addition to patties, soups and stir fries.

Preserving edible flowers

Crystallising and drying are both easy ways to preserve your edible flowers. Crystallising preserves whole flowers or individual petals with sugar to create a sparkling sweet dried flower that you can use on cakes, biscuits, drinks and desserts. Roses and violas, pansies and dianthus are my favourite flowers to crystallise. There are several ways to preserve flowers or petals, using the sugar crystallisation method.

OPTION 1 EGG WHITE: Beat an egg white to the point of tiny bubbles, not stiff. Use a small clean paint brush to paint the flower all over with the beaten egg white; then sprinkle a light coating of caster sugar over the flower before setting on a rack to dry. Store in airtight containers.

OPTION 2 GUM ARABIC: Dissolve 4 slightly rounded teaspoons of Gum Arabic (purchase online or at cake decorating shops) in 25 ml vodka. Use a small clean paintbrush to paint the flowers all over with the Gum Arabic mixture. Sprinkle over caster sugar and leave to dry before storing in airtight containers.

Dried petals and flowerfetti

Drying will preserve flowers longer than crystallisation. Dried flower petals look like confetti, hence the name flowerfetti. To dehydrate small flowers or petals, select tiny perfect buds or pull petals from the flower heads and cut off any bitter white base. Lay them in a single layer to dry. Avoid high temperatures that cook the delicate flowers. Drying times depend on each flower, the humidity and temperature. Set a dehydrator to 30°C, or use solar power on hot days but drying outside means you'll need to bring the flowers in at night. When ready, the flowers will be dry and almost crisp.

To use the flowerfetti, make flower sugar by adding the dried petals to caster sugar. It can be used to dip the rim of a glass as I've done with the elderflower fizz on page 92. Dried petals or petal sugar are lovely in cake batters or as a sprinkle over biscuits and cupcakes.

Successful dried flowers include dahlia petals, cornflowers, violas, calendula, chamomile, sunflower and rose. Store them in an airtight container out of light. Avoid drying elderflower and feijoa as they turn brown.

Freezing flowers

If I have a class or guests coming over, I will dash out into the garden the day before and pick flowers for very effective floral ice cubes. The ice cubes look pretty in a glass of something bubbly or floral cordials. As the ice melts, you're left with the floating flower. Most flowers retain their colour for up to a week before fading. Of note, is borage. While the little star shaped flower is gorgeous, it does not keep its colour well. After a day or two encased in ice, the blue colour fades dramatically.

TO MAKE FLORAL ICE CUBES

Use water that has been boiled and cooled several times. The ice blocks will have minimal oxygen and be free from the tiny air bubbles that cloud the finished effect.

Select perfect blooms or leaves for each ice cube segment and sit them into the ice cube tray. Partly fill the ice cube segments with boiled water and freeze. Once frozen, top up the ice cube with cool, boiled water and freeze again. This way the flower will be encased within the ice, frozen in time.

A FLORAL ICE BOWL

Start two days before this is needed. Select a handful of edible leaves and flowers, such as roses, sunflowers, mint leaves, verbena or lotus petals.

Choose two freezer-proof bowls that will sit inside each other with a few centimeters to spare. Place some flowers and leaves in the base of the larger bowl and top with some small ice blocks to keep the flowers in position. Put the smaller bowl on top of the flowers in the larger bowl. Weigh the small bowl down with a can of food. Pour a little water between the bowls to fill the space by one third. Freeze 12 hours. Repeat this two more times to complete the ice bowl.

Once frozen, remove the weight from the inside bowl. Pour warm water into the inside bowl to release it from the ice. Remove the outer bowl from the ice by running the outside of the bowl under a tap. You now have a beautiful floral ice bowl ready to use.

Maximising your garden space

SHADE

Do you have a shaded garden? There are plenty of options for you with edible flowers. Begonias of many types will flourish. Bedding and Angel Wings begonias are simply gorgeous. They thrive in a shaded garden bed in warmer areas such as the tropics and subtropics. In these gardens, provide them with a cool, moist root run. They require more sun in cooler climes. Violets, violas and forget-me-nots will thank you for some shade. Pansies and violas last longer in a hot climate if they have sun relief. Grow gingers in the tropics. The torch ginger tolerates some shade and is tall and skinny for a narrow side garden.

VERTICAL SPACE

Cooks and gardeners with limited space can be very savvy about utilizing every nook and cranny. Think of vertical as well as horizontal spaces. You can grow edible flowers in hanging baskets to take advantage of the views at eye height. Plant creepers, or climbers like climbing beans and peas with edible flowers, over trellises and fences for a stunning display. Even snow peas, zucchini and pumpkins can be grown vertically if space is limited.

BASKETS

If you have a verandah, hanging baskets will be beautiful when filled with blooms. Consider growing chamomile, calendula, violas and nasturtiums as they all do well in baskets where they can trail attractively over the basket rim. Regular liquid fertilisation with a combined seaweed and fish solution, will keep them performing well and producing plenty of blooms to eat and admire.

EDGES AND BORDERS

Garden bed edges and borders are an ideal spot for edibles that provide colour and food. Pansies, calendulas and forget-me-nots are sweet little border plants. A more formal edge of dwarf lavenders is lovely to behold.

Edible flower gardens

Edible flowers make a magnificent display in a dedicated garden bed. Why not consider incorporating them in other ways throughout your garden too? Here are some suggestions for putting them to good use throughout your garden.

In our garden, edible flowers provide a delightful multitude of joys, not just on the dinner plate. Flowers provide natural aromatherapy benefits. It's amazing how a fragrant bloom can change your whole mood! And not least of all, edible flowers enliven our herb terrace with a mass of joyous colour in a kaleidoscope of blooms throughout the year.

You can interplant existing shrubs with edible flowers. You can pop in some seeds or seedlings of annuals, like pansies for winter and spring colour, or tuck some dwarf dahlia bulbs amongst the foliage for a pop of summer colour. Do not mix edibles with poisonous plants in case of mistakes!

COMPANION PLANTS

Companion plants are grown for many reasons. They can help to keep insects at bay, encourage predators and bees, or they can increase soil fertility if they are nitrogen fixing legumes such as peas.

In an orchard, companion edible flowers for fruit trees include German Chamomile, borage, cornflowers and calendulas. They often self sow from the seeds they drop, giving you free edible flowers next season. Each of these attracts bees for pollination and predators to minimise pests.

In a vegetable garden, French Marigolds and calendulas produce valuable winter colour. The yellow coloured petals help to attract aphids to them rather than to your prized broccoli. Marigolds are planted to reduce root knot nematodes around tomatoes. Edible blooms are also aesthetically pleasing. Climbing roses and Blue Butterfly Vine, contribute a wonderful elegance to a garden if adorning the perimeter fence or arch.

If you love the misty romance of cottage gardens, why not plant edible flowers in profusion? In warm climates, gingers and Sambac Jasmine make a beautiful backdrop to a cottage display. Daylilies are spectacular as mid-height plants in spring and summer. Dianthus and carnations are neat, traditional border plants.

A small space flower plot

It is possible to have your own garden of edible flowers as a feature, even in a small space. A small garden bed edged with pavers can create a wonderful, seasonal colour-coded display. Paver garden edges make for easy maintenance, as they reduce the infiltration of any adjoining grass into the bed.

Large beds devoted to edible flowers may not be within the realms of all gardeners. However, the half circle garden bed in the shape of a rising sun, pictured below, is very much an 'Australian' theme and will economise on space.

This is a small bed for springtime planting, but seasonal plantings throughout the year could create a beautiful palette of colour and edibles for you.

A seasonal 'sunrise bed' incorporating edible flowers in a small space.　　　　　1m

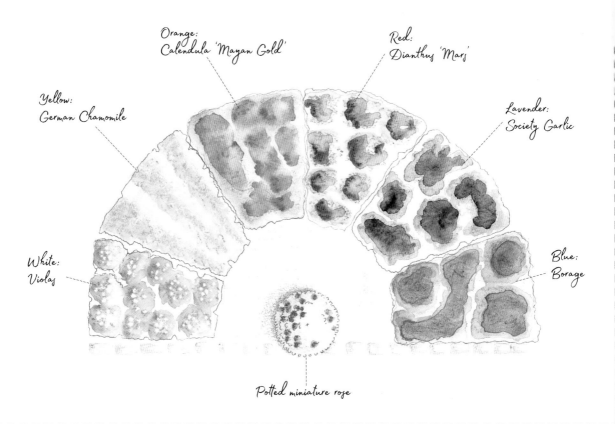

Orange:
Calendula 'Mayan Gold'

Red:
Dianthus 'Mars'

Yellow:
German Chamomile

Lavender:
Society Garlic

White:
Violas

Blue:
Borage

Potted miniature rose

An edible flower and herb garden

It's often the case that herbs and edible flowers grow together beautifully. The planting design on this page is for a culinary herb and flower garden with year-round interest. All the herbs included in this planting have edible flowers.

Our culinary herb terrace combines edible flowers with herbs in a spot I visit often. I positioned it right near the kitchen door. A permaculture rule is that the foods used most are closest to the kitchen. This simple permaculture design rule works well for us, providing food, fragrance and colour.

An edible flower and herb garden

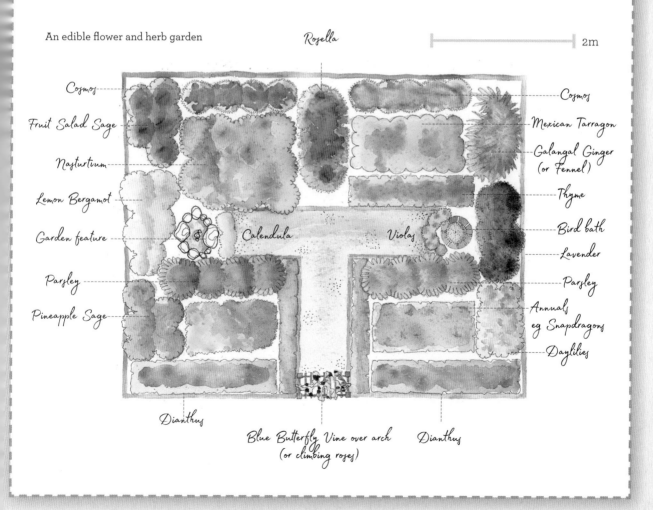

Rosella

2m

Cosmos

Fruit Salad Sage

Nasturtium

Lemon Bergamot

Garden feature

Parsley

Pineapple Sage

Calendula

Violas

Cosmos

Mexican Tarragon

Galangal Ginger (or Fennel)

Thyme

Bird bath

Lavender

Parsley

Annuals eg Snapdragons

Daylilies

Dianthus

Blue Butterfly Vine over arch (or climbing roses)

Dianthus

Growing organically

There are so many chemicals in the environment, bathing us from before birth. We do not need more applied to our food. To grow organically means you will harvest health-giving, clean produce that has no chemical fungicides, herbicides or pesticides that damage people or the environment. I am very careful to only use products that carry the Certified Organic logo or that are completely natural, such as worm castings and compost.

It is important that the flowers we eat are grown with as little chemical application as possible, from seed to harvest and serving. Studies of honey bee pollen have found high levels of hazardous chemical toxins in pollen from plants sprayed with herbicides, fungicide and pesticides. Plants that have been sprayed before or after flowering can accumulate toxins. The flowers and pollen will develop with toxins in place.

4 tips for healthy organic flowers
1. Avoid growing annuals out of season. They will be stressed by adverse conditions and will attract more pests and disease
2. Plant the right plant in the right spot. Choose the place for your flowers based upon their sun and shade needs and moisture requirements
3. Trim your flower buds off until the plant has achieved a robust size and fullness. Only then, allow it to flower
4. Inspect plants regularly for pests and disease. Spray with organic treatments only if absolutely necessary. Check for a witholding period prior to harvest.

GROWER'S NOTE: The ecological balance in your garden is fine-tuned by the ecosystem services offered by birds, frogs, lizards and insects. Where nature needs a hand, I use 'soft' organic options to control insects and disease. These products meet the Australian National Organic Standard. Gardeners can access a wide range of organic seeds, rare edible plants, gardening books, non-toxic pest control & good tools from Green Harvest Organic Gardening Supplies **www.greenharvest.com.au**

Growing in pots

A beautiful pot of edible flowers can brighten up your outdoor area and can be just as gorgeous and useful as a garden bed of flowers. A challenge for growing in pots is that they dry out more quickly and need more frequent watering and fertilising. A group of flowering edibles in pots is pretty and practical if you're renting, if you have a balcony, or you simply want to jazz up a paved area.

An advantage is that pots can also be moved around to catch the sun. Consider purchasing nifty pot castors when you are making up your pots. They make it easier for moving the potted plants around and reduce the need for lifting.

- Start with a good-sized pot so there's plenty of space for roots to develop. I generally use a pot the size of a hug. (That's my term for a pot about as large as you can cuddle in your arms.) A glazed pot doesn't lose water as does a porous terracotta one. Plastic pots are also fine to use

- Use a Certified Organic potting mix. It will contain organic certified fertilisers that will feed your plants for a short time. When potting plants, I mix in an additional sprinkle of organic fertiliser and a handful of coconut peat to help hold more moisture and feed the flowers generously. I find Organic Xtra, a pelletised manure-based product, to be excellent
- Seeds may be sown into the potting mix. Keep them moist for successful germination
- After planting seedlings, top the pot with some straw or coconut fibre as a mulch to conserve water
- A fortnightly foliar feed over the leaves and soil, from a watering can or spray bottle will support wonderful lush growth and bright flowers. Choose a fertiliser containing both fish and seaweed. They provide a wide range of beneficial nutrients for your plants
- Tuck a saucer under the pot. This simple action helps to keep the soil moist and it deters ants. Be vigilant and keep the plants well hydrated. Dry plants are stressed plants.

Six essentials for sensational soil

Healthy soil provides the perfect growing medium for healthy plants and beautiful blooms. I am a firm believer that to produce great plants you need to start by creating soil that is almost good enough to eat! Sadly, not all of us are blessed with rich, fertile topsoil. Our own garden started as heavy yellow clay and stones. After four years, I am now quite happy with the improvements that have created an easily-cultivated dark soil. You will succeed in creating a more productive garden with continued attention to building soil quality.

I maintain a strictly organic regime in our whole garden. I am confident we will be growing and eating the best. Here are six basics to keep in mind when preparing your soil to grow edible flowers successfully.

1. Test the pH of your soil regularly
2. Encourage a living soil, abounding with worms, beneficial soil microflora and microfauna. These are the millions of beneficial bacteria, fungi and life forms present in every teaspoon of healthy living soil. They live with the plant in a symbiotic relationship around the roots, feeding and protecting the plant in return for the sugars the plant exudes from healthy roots. Using organic products, natural manures, home-made compost, pictured above left, and worm castings will encourage these microscopic workers
3. Add liquid or powdered humic acid, also called humates, to hold moisture and fertility in the soil. I notice significantly less powdery mildew in the garden when I apply humates to the soil when preparing a bed for planting. Add humates when preparing the beds and then seasonally
4. Avoid herbicides, like glyphosate, which kill weeds, plants and your soil life. Hand pull or hoe weeds such as chickweed, and compost them instead. Organic alternatives to glyphosate for soft weeds are available from some nurseries. They are based on pelargonic acid or horticultural vinegar

5. Apply manures, or pelletised fertilisers, together with compost and worm liquid from your worm farm to enhance the life of the soil. The soil life will convert the fertiliser to a readily available form for the plants. I use Organic Xtra, a pelletised blend of composted manure, blood and bone, fish meal and seaweed. Apply it at soil preparation time and every 3-4 months under the mulch in perennial flower beds

6. Spread mulch after planting. It regulates soil moisture and temperature and reduces weeds. A plant-derived mulch breaks down relatively quickly, giving life and organic matter back to the soil. My locally available organic mulch of choice is sugar cane. You'll be sure to find a similar product in your area.

pH testing your soil

Make it a habit to pH test your soil at 6-12 month intervals. Nurseries have easy-to-use test kits. I aim for a slightly acidic pH 6.5 in most of my flower growing areas and vegetable beds. Add lime or dolomite if your soil pH test is acidic (below pH 6.5). They help 'sweeten' or alkalinize your soil while also adding calcium for plant cellular strength.

Add sulphur and soil microbes if your soil is alkaline (above pH 7.0). Soil microbes are abundant in fresh worm casting and liquid, in good compost, or as a microbial brew from some specialist companies.

Here are the steps for a pH test.

1. Dig down 10cm into the soil and collect a little soil on a trowel
2. Add 1 teaspoon of soil to the white plate from the kit
3. Drip about 10 drops of the pH dye indicator onto the soil. Stir it to create a chocolate icing consistency
4. Puff the barium powder over the wet soil. Wait 1 minute (do not stir) and compare the colour of the barium to the chart. This is the pH of your soil

Buying seedlings

Buying seedlings means you have about a 4-6 week head start on sowing from seed. However, unless you purchase organically raised seedlings, they will most likely have been treated with chemicals such as non-organic fertilisers, fungicides or pesticides.

Here are four suggestions to minimise chemical exposure when you cannot purchase organically grown seedlings.

1. Buy the smallest seedlings you can as they have had less exposure to chemicals
2. Dip them in a tub of diluted eco-seaweed solution when you get them home from the nursery
3. At planting time, remove the seedlings from the punnets and swish the soil off the roots in the seaweed solution
4. Gently plant them into organic potting mix or garden soil. Water in well with a fresh watering can of eco-seaweed. Trim off all flowers and buds. The plant will now have a reduced chemical load as it grows.

Saving seeds

I prefer to grow heirloom varieties that have been grown for sometimes hundreds of years, for their resilience and reliability rather than hybridised plants. I enjoy the link with past generations and the variety of heirloom plants available.

If you allow plants to produce seed, collect the seed to sow for next season. Allow the pods to dry on the plant then snip them off. Dry the pods, or flower heads, in a paper bag for a week or so before separating them. Keep only the seed, not the chaff.

Store the seeds in tiny, labelled, ziplock bags once completely dry. Keep the packs in a dark, cool place ready to re-sow next season. This way you get free plants. Search online for seed suppliers if you don't collect your own. I use **greenharvest.com.au**.

Sowing seeds

Growing from seed is a satisfying and economical way to grow your food. For some, growing from seed can seem a bit scary at first – is that you? Once you get the hang of it you will be rewarded with a wonderful range of flowers that you may never have had access to as seedlings. You can save your own seed and share it with others. The growing chart on pages 155-156 indicates the seasons for sowing and harvesting your flowers.

I often start seeds in the finished worm castings from a worm farm. Here are the steps to sowing seeds in worm castings.

i.   Remove the top layer of the worm farm with the castings in it
ii.   Separate out the worms and worm eggs. Start a new layer for your worm farm with these
iii.   Dry the castings out to kill the remaining worm eggs as worms in seed trays are not desirable
iv.   Fluff the castings with a hand fork and fill seedling trays. Smooth the surface
v.   Sow seed in rows, into the pure casting. Keep this little seed bed moist. A dry period at germination will kill or severely impact upon your seeds.

If you don't have worm castings, fill small pots or seedlings trays with a fine-grained organic potting mix. To make your own: mix 6 parts coconut coir peat; 1 part vermiculite or perlite; 1 part composted bark fines (sieve the bark to make it finer); 3 parts washed sand; 1 part fine organic fertiliser.

Some flower seeds such as violas, are miniscule. I find that mixing them with a little sand helps to sow them more evenly. Larger seeds such as sunflowers, can be sown directly into the spot they are to grow. Water thoroughly, using a fine droplet to prevent the seeds dislodging. Boost germination by using fulvic acid or eco-seaweed at this first watering. Transplant into the garden when they have grown 3-4 leaves. Surround each with a small pot, with the base cut out, to protect the young seedlings from predators.

GROWER'S NOTE: Green Harvest Organic Gardening Supplies are my preferred place to buy organic seeds. You'll find a wonderful range of certified organic, open pollinated, untreated, non-hybrid, GMO free and heirloom seeds and other gardening essentials in their on-line store. **www.greenharvest.com.au**

Reducing plant stress

It's important to keep plants stress free to achieve the most delicious and showy results. Plants that are stressed from heat or drought will produce dull flowers that may be bitter and chewy. So, keep your plants well-watered from germination right through to harvest.

WATERING TIME

Should you water in the morning or the evening? There are two arguments. Some say watering at night will encourage fungal disease as the water stays on the leaf overnight. This can create ideal fungal growth conditions. In cold areas, the water can freeze on the leaves or blooms causing damage. The other school of thought, especially for hot areas, is that evening watering is best. The water is applied to the cooler soil and will have all night to hydrate the plant.

I recommend doing what suits you and your climatic conditions. We live in the subtropics, so I water in the late afternoon or early evening. However, if your plants are drooping and wilting, water them when they need it, rather than waiting.

HEAT AND COLD STRESS

Include a fortnightly foliar feed with eco-seaweed to reduce heat or cold stress. For large gardens, make up a more concentrated seaweed solution in a click-on hose container and spray the whole garden in a flash. You will see the leaves change to look more robust when eco-seaweed is used.

GROWER'S NOTE: Most seaweed products are plant health tonics, not fertilisers. Seaweed alone lacks high enough levels of nitrogen, phosphorous and potassium to achieve the 'fertiliser' tag.

Fertilising for fabulous flowers

I find a balanced fertiliser that supplies nitrogen, phosphorous, potassium, sulphur and micronutrients, gets the best result from our edible flowers. A good fertiliser is like a well-rounded diet. Phosphorous and potassium are both needed to stimulate blooming and flower colour. I add a dusting of pulverised ash from the cob oven to the soil annually. It's a source of potash and also helps to regulate the pH of acid soils.

PELLETISED FERTILISER

Pelletised manure-based fertilisers are applied to the soil when preparing for planting. Organic Xtra is a well-rounded fertiliser that I use in all garden beds. As the plants grow, nurture them with fortnightly foliar feeds using a liquid feed.

USING WORM LIQUID

Some people swear by diluted worm liquid as a foliar feed. It will burn your plants if used too strongly or if it is not fresh. It is only as nutritionally rich as the diet you feed your worms. I prefer to use worm liquid as a soil addition rather than a leaf application, especially for edible blooms. Worm liquid is rich in microbes that I am not too keen to eat with my flowers.

LIQUID FERTILISERS

Liquid fertilisers, used as foliar applications through a sprayer, are essential for your blooming garden. An organic fertiliser containing fish plus seaweed, sprayed onto to the leaves fortnightly will be absorbed into the plant in about twenty minutes. It's like giving them a super charged meal. Liquid fertilisers, like eco-aminogro, help to protect plants like roses, zucchini and summer blooms from humidity-induced fungal attack.

Organic pest control

Your flowers can be a tempting meal for insects. A few insects in the garden may be OK, but there can be nothing worse than seeing a caterpillar crawling on your flower-decorated cake! Your planned delicate spray of roses can be spoilt by an overnight infestation of aphids. A few hungry furry or feathered friends can eat up a whole patch of flowers quick smart.

It can be easy to reach for the spray bottle of poison for a quick eradication. But avoid this on your flowers. So, without poisoning yourself or the environment, try these organic methods to help reduce pest numbers on your flowers.

SNAILS AND SLUGS
These hungry devils travel by night and chew at new seedlings, buds and fresh petals. To control them you can do several things:

- Dust affected plants and surrounds with food grade diatomaceous earth
- Pick them off and feed them to the chooks
- For pots, encircle the top of the pot with horticultural copper tape. Slugs and snails won't pass over it.

BIRDS
In our garden, cockatoos and corellas can decimate our flowers. Cover your precious plants with fine weave netting similar to shade cloth. This can prevent damage but also prevents wildlife entanglement. I have been known to sleep out in the hammock before key events in our garden just to keep the cockatoos away from the sunflowers. Call me crazy...

CATERPILLARS
Caterpillars can be very pretty and we all know they form into butterflies or moths. A couple of them here and there are manageable to pick off by hand. If they are too numerous, food grade diatomaceous earth is effective for caterpillar control. A fine dusting is all you need. Reapply when it washes off with rain or irrigation.

SCALE INSECTS

There are many types of scale, from dry, to waxy. Scale insects are tiny sap suckers that cover themselves in a protective coating. They love the sweet plant juices from new growth. Ants carry scale insects onto the plants, collecting the sweet exudation called honeydew. They feed this to their young. If you see ants on your edible plants, suspect scale or aphids. Dry scale is commonly found on rose stems (pictured at right). It looks white and flaky. Scrub these off with hot soapy water and a nail brush, then apply eco-oil. Wax scales appear on stems and leaves near veins. Wipe off as much scale as possible then apply eco-oil. You will need several applications as instructed on the pack.

APHIDS

Aphids are ½ to 1mm sized green or brown insects that mass onto new tips and shoots. A range of control methods can be used to deter or treat them. Aphids usually appear at times of active plant growth, sucking the sweet juices from the plant. Ants tend to aphids for the sweet exudates. Kill the aphids and the ants will disappear.

- Squirt aphids with a jet of water from the hose to dislodge them
- Spray with horticultural soap spray to kill the pests
- Companion plant around the susceptible plants with onions, chives or Society Garlic
- Apply an organic oil spray such as eco-oil. Spray right down the stem of the plant to the base.

POSSUMS

I have tried chilli sprays on foliage to deter possums, but they ignore the spiciness. I find that physical barriers work best.
- Create wire baskets to cover pots or plants. Secure into position with tent pegs or a bamboo stake and cover the end to prevent injury.
- A floppy fence works well. I find possums avoid climbing something that wiggles around. We use temporary walls of old fly screens, staked around susceptible plants for protection.
- An electric fence also works wonders. Our 'chook net' fence goes up around a whole bed if possum pressure is great.

Allergies

Most flowers have pollen, which is essential for plant reproduction and many have an abundance of pollen. It's a particular design ploy by nature to create the best opportunities for fertilisation and sharing of genetic material between plants.

The daisy family that includes sunflowers, chamomile, zinnias and calendulas, reveals the pollen on open discs with the petals arranged around the reproductive organs and pollen bearing structures. They are typically heavy pollen bearers as are male zucchini and male pumpkin flowers, and daylilies. When preparing flowers with large pollen-coated stamens, remove the stamens by snapping them off or cutting them away with small scissors. The pollen is often bitter and can spoil the flavour of a dish. Rinse or wipe the flowers to remove pollen remnants as you prepare them.

Pollen can cause allergic reactions in those who are sensitive to it. Asthmatics and hay fever sufferers may react to pollen on edible flowers, so do check sensitivities before eating or serving edible flowers. I avoid serving high pollen whole flowers such as chamomile (pictured) to allergy sufferers. Safer options include flowers like beans and peas that have a tiny amount of pollen and have already been self-fertilised before they open.

Some serious don'ts
- Don't eat flowers from florists
- Don't eat flowers from roadsides or parklands
- Don't eat flowers that are sprayed or grown conventionally
- All of these may be laced with pesticides and other nasties.

Tempting but toxic

A note about your flower garden. Growing poisonous flowers in amongst edible blooms should be avoided at all costs. The risk of mistakenly harvesting poisonous flowers along with your edibles is just too great. For example, foxgloves in your vegetable garden are deadly, so plant edible but equally lovely hollyhocks instead.

This is a short list of some poisonous flowers commonly grown in Australian gardens. There are many more flowers that are tempting but toxic. Take care to identify your flowers accurately before eating them. If you have any doubts, it's safest to leave them out of your mouth.

A good reference for Australian gardeners is 'Pretty but Poisonous: plants poisonous to people: An illustrated guide for Australia', by R.C.H Shepherd. Melbourne 2004.

SOME COMMONLY GROWN POISONOUS FLOWERS

Common Names	Botanical name	Common Names	Botanical name
Allamanda	*Allamanda cathartica* species	Irises	*Iris* species
Agapanthus	*Agapanthus* species	Lantana	*Lantana camira*
Angel's Trumpet	*Daytura & Brugmansia* species	Oleander	*Nerium oleander*
Arum Lily	*Zantedeschia aethiopica*	Peruvian Lilies	*Alstromeria aurea*
Carolina Jessamine	*Gelsemium sempervirens*	Poinsettia	*Euphorbia pulcherrima*
Cunjevoi	*Alocasia macrorrhizos*	Rhododendrons & Azaleas	*Rhododendron* species
Daffodil	*Narcissus* species	Silky Oak	*Grevillea robusta*
Duranta, Sheena's Gold Geisha Girl	*Duranta erecta & Duranta repens*	Snow in Summer	*Cerastium tomentosum*
Dwarf Elder	*Sambucus ebulus*	Sweet Peas	*Lathyrus odoratus*
Foxglove	*Digitalis purpurea & species*	White Cedar	*Melia azadarach*
Frangipani	*Plumeria* species	Wisteria	*Wisteria sinensis, W. floribunda*
Hydrangea	*Hydrangea macrophylla*	Yesterday, Today and Tomorrow	*Brunfelsia bonodora*

Banana Bell, Banana flower
Musa species

GROWING: Bananas are our tallest perennial herbs. The flowers form when the banana plant is eleven to fourteen months old. It begins with a bell on a long stem. The bell is a bract of bright leathery flower 'scales' that protect layers of yellow tubular flowers. It's these little yellow flowers that form into bananas. The edible bell is at the terminal end of the fruiting stem.

Bananas need moist, fertile, well-drained soil, pH 6.5, enriched with plenty of dolomite, potassium, compost and manure to produce healthy bunches. Sink plants 10-20 cm deep into soil. Provide the banana plant with 2-3 monthly applications of organic fertiliser such as Organic Xtra. Provide a light sprinkle of potash or charcoal around the root zone as the bell emerges. Grow extra clumps from your own thin, sword-shaped suckers as these produce the best parent plants.

Home growers no longer require a special permit to grow bananas in Queensland. Buy plants only from registered growers such as Blue Sky Backyard Bananas to assist in maintaining a disease-free banana industry.

HARVESTING AND EDIBLE PARTS: Some bananas such as Gold Finger and Lady Finger have a sweeter bell than others. Once the banana flower has developed all its green bananas, cut off the bell at the end of the bunch. It's now ready for kitchen preparation. I have a short video on how to prepare the banana bell at **www.ecobotanica.com.au/videos**

Some people cook the tiny yellow flowers. These are time consuming to prepare as each flower must have its stamens removed prior to cooking.

COLOUR:	Dark purplish red
SUN/SHADE:	Full sun
PLANTING:	Suckers or tissue-cultured plants in warm seasons
FLOWERING:	All year in tropics; summer to autumn in the subtropics
HEIGHT:	2-5 m tall

GROWER'S NOTE

Did you know Bananas are the world's most popular fruit? Each 'tree' produces one bunch of bananas and one bell. Remove the bell after the bananas have fully formed to encourage fruit size. Keep the bell and make the delicious meal on the next page.

Devika's seeni sambol with Banana Bell

The banana bell is most delicious when properly prepared and cooked to remove its bitterness. Devika, a Sri Lankan friend, introduced me to this delicious, deeply fragrant banana bell recipe. It's well worth the effort.

MAKES 1 CUP GF, V, DF

BANANA FLOWER
1 banana bell
(about 2 cups of shreds)
1 tablespoon salt
1 teaspoon grated turmeric

SPICE PASTE
3 green cardamom pods
4 cloves
2 tablespoons fresh mild red chilli pieces
2 fresh lemon grass stems
(pound the white part then finely snip with scissors)
1 tablespoon dulse flakes
(a seaweed substitute for Maldive fish)

CURRY SPICES
1 teaspoon gluten free roasted Sri Lankan curry powder
2 tablespoons olive oil
6 fresh or dried curry leaves
2 teaspoons brown sugar
½ teaspoon tamarind paste
salt to taste

BELL PREPARATION: Wash the bell, remove the strong stem, the tough red 'petals' (aka bracts) removing the little yellow flowers between the remaining petals as they can be bitter. Peel down to the inner paler bell. Slice the bell into shreds about ¼ cm thick. Soak shreds in a bowl of water for at least 30 minutes with 1 tablespoon of salt and the grated turmeric.

SPICE PASTE: Use a mortar and pestle to crush the cardamom pods to release the seeds. Discard the papery pods, keep the seeds and add the cloves to the cardamom seeds. Crush them both to a powder. Add the chilli, lemon grass and dulse flakes and crush to a paste. Add a teaspoon or two of water if the mix is very dry.

Drain the banana bell, rinse thoroughly under running water then squeeze out the excess water using your hands.

Toss the curry powder into a saucepan and turn the heat to medium. Dry roast it until fragrant. Remove from the heat to cool a little before adding the olive oil, curry leaves and spice paste. Stir over moderate heat for 30 seconds. Add the bell shreds, brown sugar and tamarind paste. Cook over low heat, stirring often until soft. Add a little water periodically to give it some moisture as it cooks, but don't add too much as this is meant to be fairly dry. Cooking time is 40-50 minutes depending on heat and shred size.

Taste for salt and add if needed. Serve with rice.

Bean and pea flowers
Phaseolus species (beans) *Pisum sativum* (peas)

GROWING: Many beans will grow and flower in frost free, coastal and subtropical areas throughout the year. Bush beans, French Beans and Dwarf Borlotti are prolific producers on compact bushes. Most bush beans are annuals, giving two harvests before dying off. Save the best pods to dry on the bush and collect them for sowing next season.

For space saving climbing beans, try 'Purple King' with purple flowers and perennial wing beans with white flowers. Wing bean seeds germinate once night time temperatures reach at least 15°C. They grow up a tall support and flower as the days shorten in autumn.

Sugar snaps, snow peas and purple podded peas are prolific flowerers. Purple-podded peas produce bright purple flowers followed by delightful pods.

Grow beans and peas from seed. Sow each seed directly into fertiliser-enriched soil with a sprinkle of lime. Sow about 1-2 cm deep. For climbing beans and peas, set up a 2-3 metre tall trellis before planting so they can reach for the sky.

HARVESTING AND EDIBLE PARTS: The flowers may be eaten fresh or cooked. Large blue bean flowers will lose colour within hours, but flowers from climbing beans and bush beans retain their colour and crispness in the fridge for 3-4 days. Pick large blue bean flowers (eg. from cow peas as in the picture, close to serving time.)

COLOUR: White through to purple

SUN/SHADE: Full sun

PLANTING: Seeds-generally spring through autumn

FLOWERING: Most beans: spring to summer; Borlotti beans-winter; Wing and soy beans-summer; Peas-winter and spring

HEIGHT: Bush beans 30-40 cm; Climbing peas and beans- 2 to 3 m on trellis

GROWER'S NOTE: Poison Beans. DO NOT eat the pretty flowers of the climbing Yam bean, also known as Jicama (*Pachyrhizus erosus tuberosus*). All parts of the plant except the swollen root are poisonous. Processed plant parts become the potent insecticide Rotenone.

Bean flower salad with ginger jellies

Bean flowers are a key crunchy ingredient in this salad. They can be used in other dishes as a delicious garnish, in vegetarian patties and can be snipped into salad sandwiches for extra zing. Make the jellies first. They keep up to three days in the fridge. They complement the salad beautifully.

SERVES 6 GF, V, DF

ORANGE AND GINGER JELLIES
30 g fresh ginger root
300 ml fresh orange juice
300 ml clear apple and pear juice
1 pinch hot chilli powder or a
slice or two of fresh hot chilli
Pinch salt
20 g agar agar powder
½ cup water

SALAD
1 cup green beans sliced into
long fine slices
1 cup fresh bean or pea flowers
3 cups firm (green) papaya,
peeled and julienned or shredded
1 cup carrot, grated or julienned
½ cup cherry tomatoes, quartered
1 spring onion sliced thinly
½ cup Thai basil leaves

DRESSING
½ cup coconut vinegar
1 tablespoon lime juice
1 teaspoon diced chilli
3 teaspoons coconut sugar or
brown sugar
1 teaspoon tamari soy
1 clove garlic, crushed

ORANGE AND GINGER JELLIES: Scrub clean and then finely grate the ginger root. Put it into a small piece of muslin or cheesecloth and twist it into a bundle. Squeeze the juice out, catching it in a saucepan. Add the fruit juices, chilli and salt to the saucepan. Bring to the boil and reduce the juices to almost half. Remove from the heat and cool for two minutes. Strain through a fine sieve.

Dissolve the agar in ½ cup cool water. Whisk it into the juice mixture. It will only set once boiled, so reheat the mixture and simmer 30 seconds. Remove from the heat. Pour into a lightly oiled 10 x 15 cm pyrex dish or cake tin and set in the fridge. Once set, cut into small cubes.

SALAD AND DRESSING: Blanch the green beans in boiling water 30 seconds. Drain and cool off. Combine all salad ingredients in a large bowl. Shake the dressing ingredients together in a jar and drizzle over the salad.

Serve with Orange and Ginger Jellies.

Begonia
Begonia species

GROWING: Begonias thrive in humus-rich soil that is evenly moist. Harsh summer sun will burn them, so provide a shady spot or grow under a tree for best results. Bedding begonias grow to 10-30 cm and will tolerate more sun, but keep the water up to them. They are frost tender, so provide a protected spot for perennial growth.

I fertilise and mulch my begonias 3-4 times per year with an organic pelletised fertiliser and they get an occasional foliar feed of seaweed and fish fertiliser. This also helps to keep them free of fungal disease.

HARVESTING AND EDIBLE PARTS: Crisp and waxy, begonia flowers have been used in cooking since Victorian times. All begonia flowers are edible although not all are palatable. Common species you will find include the Wax Begonias - *Begonia cucullita* (was *B. semperflorens*) and Tuberous Begonias – *B. tuberhybrida*. I recommend you have a tiny sample taste first as some petals can be bitter.

My favourite begonia flowers are the Tree or Cane Begonias, also known as Angel Wing Begonias (*B. coccinea*). They flower in the subtropics almost all year and have a crisp lemony flavoured flower.

Begonias originate in the Atlantic forests of Central and Southern America. They have been cultivated for at least 1400 years and have been eaten and used in herbal remedies as astringents, to clean wounds and to reduce swelling.

COLOUR: A wide range of colours including pastels, white, red, orange

SUN/SHADE: Part shade

PLANTING: Cuttings-spring to autumn

FLOWERING: Most of the year in the subtropics

HEIGHT: Variable depends on species

GROWER'S NOTE: Begonia petals contain some oxalic acid and should only be eaten in small amounts. If you have gout or kidney stones, eating plants containing oxalic acid can exacerbate the condition.

Floral spring rolls

If you are after something light for lunch or dinner, these floral spring rolls may be perfect for you. The flowers show through the rice paper wrapper like flowers in a window. I offered some to our builder. He was so impressed, he took pictures before eating them.

MAKES ABOUT 12 ROLLS GF, V, DF

DRESSING FOR FILLING
2 teaspoons fresh ginger
2 teaspoons palm sugar
1 tablespoon lime juice
1 dessertspoon sweet chilli sauce
1 teaspoon dulse seaweed flakes
1 teaspoon tamari soy sauce
Salt and pepper

FILLING AND ROLLS
1 small cake of rice vermicelli noodles
1 small Lebanese cucumber
½ cup packaged flavoured tofu
1 cup shredded lettuce leaves
2/3 cup grated carrot
1/3 cup diced red onion
1 pack of rice paper sheets
Begonia flowers and herbal leaves eg parsley, dill, fennel

TO SERVE: 1 quantity of Ginger flower dipping sauce on page 100.

DRESSING: Grate the ginger very finely. Add it to a bowl with the remaining ingredients and stir to combine. Set aside.

FILLING: Soak the rice vermicelli noodles in warm water for 10 minutes until soft. You will need 1 cup rehydrated noodles.

Cut the cucumber in half lengthways and scoop out the seeds. Slice into fine batons. Slice the tofu to match. Add the tofu and cucumber to a bowl with the remaining ingredients for the filling, then spoon over the dressing and mix through.

ASSEMBLY: Soak the rice paper sheets one at a time, for 20-30 seconds, in a shallow dish of water. Remove the softened sheet of rice paper from the water and place it on a clean linen tea towel. Lay a line of begonia flowers and leaves across the top third of the rice paper sheet. Put 1 dessertspoon of the filling mix across the middle third of the rice paper sheet. Fold the bottom third of the rice paper sheet to cover the filling. Fold in the sides. Finally, roll the little parcel away from you firmly. As you roll you will see the flowers and leaves rolling around to meet you, visible inside the rice paper. Repeat until the filling and sheets have been used up.

Serve with Ginger flower dipping sauce.

Blue Butterfly Vine, Bunga Telang (Malay.)
Clitoria ternatea

GROWING: The very showy Blue Butterfly Vine needs a tropical or subtropical climate with a cool root zone to grow successfully. A perennial vine, it originates in south east Asia and can be found growing throughout the tropical and subtropical regions of the world. The flat pods resemble pea pods. Once dried, the pods split open. Seeds may be sown into pots or directly into the ground during the warmer months.

It's happy scrambling over a low trellis, arch or fence. Keeping the support structure within arm's reach will allow you to harvest the attractive flowers for cooking. Ensure you have a mulch over the root zone and that the soil is moist in summer.

HARVESTING AND EDIBLE PARTS: Harvest the flowers when fresh and bright. They are the source of a natural blue food dye once cooked in water. Young seed pods are also edible when steamed.

The flowers may be dried on a biscuit rack inside and can be cooked later for food colouring. Store dried flowers in airtight jars.

Much research has been undertaken into this plant, as it's used in traditional Ayurvedic medicine. Flower uses include treatment for memory improvement. It's used in folk medicine as an antibiotic and antifungal agent and has many more applications. The anthocyanin-rich colouring changes when acids or alkaline mixtures are added to it. For this reason, it's sometimes used as a cocktail mixer.

COLOUR:	Blue. A white form is also available
SUN/SHADE:	Sun, part shade
PLANTING:	Seeds-spring to summer
FLOWERING:	Early to late summer
HEIGHT:	A twining climber that grows up to several metres tall

Blue sticky rice with caramel coconut custard

This blue sticky rice recipe is a favourite dish of many Malaysian people. The rice is flavoured with pandan leaves and coloured with blue *Clitoria ternatea* flowers, also known as Blue Butterfly Vine. Enjoy it with the creamy traditional caramel coconut custard.

SERVES 8-10 GF, V, DF

BLUE STICKY RICE
25 Blue Butterfly Vine flowers
100 ml water
3 tablespoons sugar
350 g glutinous (sticky) rice
440 ml can coconut milk
4 pandan leaves

CARAMEL COCONUT CUSTARD
3 large eggs
300 ml coconut cream
150 g granular coconut sugar
50 g extra coconut sugar
3 pandan leaves tied in knots
1 tablespoon cornflour in 1 tablespoon water

COOK'S NOTE: Glutinous (sticky) rice, frozen pandan leaf and coconut sugar are available from many supermarkets and Asian grocers. The pandan leaf plant grows well from the subtropics to tropics. If leaves are unavailable, substitute a few drops of pandan essence

COLOURING: Add the flowers to a small saucepan with water and sugar. Stir occasionally while gently heating to boiling point. The water will turn bright blue. Strain out the flowers and retain the blue water.

RICE: Divide the rice into two portions and place each in a bowl. Cover the rice in each bowl with coconut milk. Add the blue water to one bowl only. Set both portions aside in the fridge to soak for 6-8 hours.

Drain each bowl of rice of any coconut milk. Steam each portion of rice separately, adding two pandan leaves to the water under each portion of rice. Steam for about 30 minutes until the rice is cooked and sticky. When cooked, fluff each with a fork. Tip both portions of rice into a bowl and combine, creating a blue marbled effect.

Line a 20 cm square cake tin with baking parchment. Tip the rice into the tin. Firm the rice flat with wet hands. Cover and chill. Cut into pieces and serve with caramel coconut custard.

CUSTARD: Place eggs, coconut cream and 150 g coconut sugar into a blender. Blend on low speed until combined.

Put 50 g coconut sugar into a medium saucepan with 2 teaspoons water and heat, stirring constantly until sugar is melted. Stir the egg mixture into the melted sugar and add the pandan leaves. Stir over low heat until the mixture thickens and bubbles (about 15 minutes). Stir in the cornflour and water. Cook for 1 minute, stirring constantly. Remove the pandan leaves. Store in the fridge until needed.

Borage, Star Flower, Blue Borage
Boragio officinalis

GROWING: These attractive, fuzzy-leaved annuals produce a flower spike rising up to 1 metre tall. Each spike carries a number of pretty blue star-shaped flowers. Sow the seed (which looks remarkably like mouse droppings!) from late summer to late winter directly into rich, fertile soil. Seed will germinate within a fortnight.

Alternatively, sow the seed in punnets or small pots and transplant them when they have grown 2-4 leaves. Choose a warm, sunny spot for winter and early spring planting or a cooler part-shade area for warm weather planting. They will self-seed from the parent plant, so you will have little borage popping up in the surrounding garden. These may transplant to other beds successfully.

Borage hates wet roots, so good drainage in warm wet weather is essential. Stake the tall flower head with bamboo stakes and a soft tie.

Bees are attracted to borage flowers. Both our native bees and honey bees can be seen nuzzling into the flowers whenever they are blooming.

HARVESTING AND EDIBLE PARTS: Harvest the cucumber-flavoured flowers in the morning when they are still fresh and crisp. They keep in a covered container in the fridge for 2-3 days though the petals do curl as they dehydrate. Borage flowers make beautiful floral ice cubes to float in drinks. The colour only lasts about 3 days when frozen. But, the plants are so generous, it's easy to start again with a new batch. They crystallise easily for the top of summer pavlovas and meringues.

The leaves taste a little like cucumber. While the seeds are not edible, their oil is used medicinally.

COLOUR: Mid blue, some are pink or white

SUN/SHADE: Full sun to part shade

PLANTING: Seed or seedling- spring to summer

FLOWERING: Early spring through to late summer

HEIGHT: Up to 1 m x 60 cm wide

GROWERS NOTE: In 'Poisonous Plants, a handbook for Doctors, pharmacists, toxicologists, biologists and veterinarians', by Frohne and Pfnder, they recommend only occasional low dose use of the leaves due to pyrrolizidine alkaloids which can cause liver damage.

Cool as a cucumber borage smoothie bowl

This smoothie bowl is deliciously beautiful for breakfast. And, it's fresh and sugar free. The borage flowers and leaves add the freshness of cucumber to the smoothie bowl.

SERVES 2 GF, V, DF

SMOOTHIE
¼ cup washed borage leaves
½ ripe avocado
¼ cup sliced Lebanese or
Telegraph cucumber
1 cup frozen mango flesh
½ cup frozen pineapple pieces
¼ cup coconut water or almond milk

COOK'S NOTE: Borage flowers crystallise perfectly. To maximize your harvest and have some on hand when you need them, follow the directions for crystallisation on page 8.

TO SERVE: Borage flowers, pineapple, berries, cornflower granola*

Add all the ingredients except the borage flowers into a blender. The avocado will provide a delectably smooth texture. I have a high speed blender which whizzes it to silky smooth in 40 seconds. Regular blenders may be a little slower.

Blend on high speed until the leaves and icy fruits are completely broken down. Pour into bowls and top with borage flowers, fruit and granola.

*Cornflower granola is perfect in this smoothie bowl. Find the recipe on page 68.

Bougainvillea, Paper Flower, Bugambilia (Phill.)
Bougainvillea glabra

GROWING: The riotously colourful bougainvillea flowers are in fact papery leaved bracts. The true flower is tiny, yellow and star shaped in the centre of the bracts.

Bougainvilleas will lose their leaves over winter if cool and dry. A warmer, moist area will help to keep them evergreen. They need very little care once established and will grow in poor soils. They survive drought (but may lose all leaves in winter) and some varieties even tolerate a light frost. Because of their thorns which help them climb, it's best to plant them in an out-of-the-way spot where you won't be tearing your clothes when you walk by.

Bougainvilleas flower well in large planters as they enjoy root bound situations. Fertilise in late winter and again in summer with a high phosphorous, low nitrogen organic fertiliser that will encourage flowers over leaf production. Prune them lightly after flowering as heavily pruned bougainvilleas may produce more thorns and fewer flowers for a time.

HARVESTING AND EDIBLE PARTS: Harvesting the colourful bracts requires some care to avoid injury from thorns. Cut bunches with a short stem for use in the kitchen. Use the rich, dark forms such as 'Mrs Butt' to produce a natural colouring that makes brilliant drinks. A Bulgarian study* of five edible flowers has found bougainvillea to be high in antioxidant and anti-inflammatory betalain pigments. Betacyanin, one of those pigments is recognised as 'powerful antioxidants with anti-inflammatory and anticarcinogenic activity.'

The bright bracts of bougainvillea, when boiled and crushed, make a glorious food colouring. The colouring may be added to drinks, jelly, aspics or clear syrups for a brilliant glow.

COLOUR: White, pastels and bright colours but not blue

SUN/SHADE: Full sun to part shade

PLANTING: Cuttings and seed spring to autumn

FLOWERING: Summer

HEIGHT: Dwarf varieties under 1 m or tall climbers

GROWER'S NOTE:
*Ref: Five Edible Flowers – Valuable source of antioxidants in human nutrition.
IJPPR. 2016, 8(4) 604-610

Bougainvillea switzel

Switzel is an-old fashioned drink also known as 'shrub' or 'fruit vinegar'. As a teen I'd make raspberry switzel by the gallon for mum's tea shop at the local folk museum. Switzel contains apple cider vinegar, a thirst quenching addition to the drink.

MAKES ABOUT 5 CUPS OF CONCENTRATE GF, V, DF

4 cups bright, fresh, bougainvillea flower bracts
4 cups filtered water
¾ cup white sugar
4 slices of lemon
1 cup fresh lemon verbena flowers and leaves OR lemon myrtle leaves
1 cup fresh pineapple pieces
½ cup unpasteurized apple cider vinegar

COOK'S NOTE: Using unpasteurised apple cider vinegar, which has the vinegar mother, encourages the development of beneficial bacteria in a very mild ferment, so it's good for gut health. For an alcoholic switzel, add a little gin to your glass!

TO SERVE: Seasonal fruits

Rinse the bougainvillea to remove pollen before adding them and the water to a large saucepan. Bring to the boil and simmer gently until the water takes on the colour of the bracts.

Remove from the heat and strain out the bracts, retaining the liquid. Return the coloured liquid to the pot and add the sugar. Stir to dissolve then reheat to boil 1 minute to create a syrup. Turn off the heat and add the lemon slices, leaves and pineapple. Mash them with a potato masher to release the flavours of the fruit. Allow it to infuse in the syrup for 5 minutes. Strain the liquid and keep it, but discard the solids. Cool to room temperature.

Once cooled, add the vinegar and leave on the bench, covered, for 8-12 hours to begin fermentation. This will consume some of the sugar and give you a very slightly effervescent drink. Pour into bottles and refrigerate.

To serve, add ice and chopped seasonal fruits to a glass. Pour in a little switzel concentrate as you would for cordial. Dilute with soda or mineral water.

Calendula, Pot Marigold, English Marigold
Calendula officinalis

GROWING: Calendula are annual upright plants with soft leaves and multiple heads of flat daisy-like flowers with soft petals. They grow easily from seed or seedlings. Add compost plus manure-based fertiliser to the soil when preparing. A fortnightly foliar feed will promote flowering.

Plants will survive for 3-5 months. Snip off dead flower heads to encourage extended blooming.

Towards the end of the season, allow some flowers to brown on the plant so you can save the seeds for next season's planting. The seeds called achenes, resemble curious little barbed tails.

HARVESTING AND EDIBLE PARTS: Harvest the flower heads when the flower is fully open, then pluck off the petals for use. The flower has abundant pollen in its central disc. I avoid culinary exposure to this pollen by using only the petals.

The petals and pollen have been used in many cultures as an anti-inflammatory medicinal plant, food and fabric dye. It's a much cheaper alternative to saffron, without the same flavour and price tag. Calendula flowers impart a slightly smoky flavour to the dish you add them to. Add a teaspoonful to scrambled eggs and frittata or make calendula butter.

Of interest, calendula vinegar is used to treat athletes foot and sunburn. I also make calendula-infused oil and creams to soothe and treat dry skin.

COLOUR: Yellow to gold

SUN/SHADE: Full sun to part shade

PLANTING: Seed–early spring to autumn

FLOWERING: Winter to early summer

HEIGHT: 30-40 cm x 20-30 cm wide

GROWER'S NOTE: Calendula may be called marigold, but the plants are quite different. French Marigolds, *Tagetes patula* for example, are edible but have a strong aroma. They are used as companion plants for tomatoes as they repel root knot nematodes.

Calendula cheese balls with native dukka

These cheese balls are perfectly delectable little mouthfuls. You will have plenty of dukka left to dip with bread and olive oil, or to use as a crumble on vegetable bakes and crepes. Dukka is a middle eastern-style dry dip that takes two minutes to make in a food processor. It keeps in the fridge for a week.

MAKES 1 ½ CUPS GF, V, DF

NATIVE DUKKA
½ cup raw sesame seed
1 cup raw almonds
1 teaspoon salt
½ teaspoon cumin powder
4 heaped teaspoons powdered lemon myrtle leaves
Tasmanian pepper to taste

CALENDULA CHEESE BALLS
125 g cream cheese
1 cup grated tasty cheese
1 teaspoon smoked paprika
1 tablespoon diced spring onion
1 tablespoon cucumber pickles, chopped
1 teaspoon calendula petals
2 tablespoons extra calendula petals for rolling the balls

COOK'S NOTE: To make calendula butter, add 1-2 tablespoons chopped petals to 125 g soft butter and stir through gently. This butter is quite lovely to use on toasted sandwiches and baked vegetables with the dukka recipe above. Store any unused butter in the fridge.

DUKKA: Heat the sesame seeds in a frypan, stirring continually, until lightly golden and slightly fragrant. Place all ingredients, including the sesame seeds, into a food processor. Blend until all the ingredients are crumbled.

CALENDULA CHEESE BALLS: Add the ingredients for the cheese balls to a bowl, but keep aside the extra calendula petals. Combine ingredients with a fork. Roll into small balls with damp hands.

Mix ½ cup dukka with the extra calendula petals. Roll the cheese balls in this mixture. They are now ready to serve.

Chamomile, German Chamomile, Wild Chamomile
Matricaria chamomilla

GROWING: German Chamomile is a member of the huge daisy family, Asteraceae. It is the chamomile we use in chamomile tea. The leaves are fine and delicately fuzzy. Each plant grows as an annual, spreading loosely and flowering prolifically before meeting an abrupt end and falling over, having suddenly turned dry and brown. That's all completely natural in its life cycle.

To grow chamomile, select a warm, sunny spot and apply organic manures or Organic Xtra fertiliser. Sow seeds directly into the soil or plant seedlings about 75 cm apart. Water well to establish the plants. As the tiny plants grow four leaves, they can then be transplanted into areas where you want them to establish. Our chamomile is a companion for fruit trees and it flourishes in the tea garden. To encourage longevity and repeat flowering, harvest the flowers regularly with scissors. After the plant has died, leave some dried flower heads on the brown foliage for a week or two. This allows the plant to self-seed, ensuring a new crop of spontaneous seedlings next season.

HARVESTING AND EDIBLE PARTS: Harvest the flowers on the first day they are fully opened. To dry for tea, discard the stalks and dry the flower heads in an airy, dark spot for 1 week to dry completely. Store them in a sealed jar. Chamomile flowers are heavy pollen bearers. Those with allergies should avoid eating this flower or drinking chamomile tea.

Chamomile is a culinary herb and flower used as flavouring in cupcakes, shortbread, mulled wine, infused into vodka and is an ingredient in absinthe. German Chamomile flowers are used as a soothing tea, most often before bed, to induce a calm night's sleep. Chamomile can be sewn into sleep pillows for those who are not pollen sensitive and is often found in skin salves and soaps.

COLOUR: White with a yellow centre

SUN/SHADE: Full sun

PLANTING: Seed or seedling-spring

FLOWERING: Late winter-summer depending on area

HEIGHT: 40 cm

GROWER'S NOTE: Apple or Lawn Chamomile (Chamaemelum nobile) is a matting plant with small yellow daisy-like flowers. Apple Chamomile is not suitable for edible flower cultivation.

Chamomile and salted caramel bars

This is a no-bake slice for times when you need something sweet. It has a delicate chamomile flavour and you can up ante with more chamomile if you wish.

MAKES 24 SLICES GF, V, DF

BASE
1 cup raw cashews soaked in
filtered water 2 hours then
drained
½ cup quinoa flakes
12 medjool dates, pitted
¼ cup dried cranberries
¼ cup coconut oil
2 teaspoons dried chamomile
flowers
50 ml lemon juice

SALTED CARAMEL TOPPING
½ cup cacao butter, melted
½ cup nut butter eg almond,
peanut or cashew
⅓ cup mesquite powder*
½ teaspoon salt
squeeze lemon juice
⅓ cup honey

COOK'S NOTE: *Mesquite
is the powdered bean of the
leguminous Prosopis plant.
Mesquite has a pleasant caramel
flavour. It's available from health
food stores.

TO SERVE: Fresh chamomile petals

BASE: Add all the ingredients for the base to a food processor. Process in short pulses until the mixture resembles fine crumbs and begins to stick together. Line a 20 cm square tin with baking paper, taking the paper up the sides. Press the base into the tin and refrigerate while making the caramel top.

SALTED CARAMEL TOPPING: Cool the cacao butter 5 minutes. Add the nut butter, mesquite powder, salt, lemon juice and honey to the cacao butter and beat together by hand until fully combined and creamy. If it's still a little oily, add more mesquite powder two teaspoons at a time, until all the cacao butter is absorbed.

Spread over the base and chill. Cut into small bars and top with some fresh chamomile petals.

Chicory, Blue Dandelion
Cichorium intybus

GROWING: Chicory is most often grown for its bitter leaves, but the 3 cm flowers are both edible and pretty. It's a frost tolerant plant that will tolerate acidic soils to pH 4.5, but does best in soils with a pH above 5.5.

To grow chicory, sow seed directly into the garden bed with additional fertilisers such as Organic Xtra to promote abundant leaves. Chicory requires summer rain or irrigation, but in areas of high summer rain, the deep taproot may rot.

If you have chicory flowering, little seedlings spontaneously pop up along dry paths and in hot garden spots. (Let me warn you, it can be a weed.) In its first season the plant will produce a basal rosette of leaves that looks a little like dandelion. The winter leaves are the least bitter to eat. They become more bitter in summer.

Chicory is stimulated to flower after at least three weeks with temperatures that dip to 4°C. The daisy-like flowers, which are usually blue but occasionally pink or white, form on a tall stem. They open mid-morning, but only every second day in our garden.

HARVESTING AND EDIBLE PARTS: Harvest the flowers mid-morning after they have opened. Flowers will close when stored, so if you want to have open flowers, pick close to serving time and keep them in a bright spot. Flowers lose their colour within hours if refrigerated. The whole flowers, like sunflowers, have a large disc with pollen in the middle, so you may only want to use the petals.

They are not often seen as part of edible flower punnets as the flowers close daily. They are beautiful home grown edible flowers and may be used in pasta dishes, sauces and salads.

COLOUR: Blue, pink, white

SUN/SHADE: Full sun

PLANTING: Seed-autumn to spring

FLOWERING: Late autumn to summer

HEIGHT: 1.5 m

GROWER'S NOTES: Chicory flowers are incorporated into homeopathic Bach Flower Remedies and have been used in folk medicine for the treatment of gallstones and gastro.

When flower stalks form, stake them to provide support for the stem.

Chicory flower salad, blue vein dressing and candied pecans

Even though they sound similar, chicory and chick peas are not related botanically, but they do match well as a bitter herb salad with the rich flavour of a blue cheese dressing. The type of blue cheese you use will determine its pungency. The pecans, candied with rosemary, are sensational in this salad.

SERVES 6-8 GF, V

CANDIED PECANS
2 teaspoons butter
1 tablespoon white sugar
50 g pecans
1 teaspoon finely snipped rosemary leaves and flowers

DRESSING
½ cup Greek yoghurt
½ cup crème fraiche or sour cream
1 dessertspoon olive oil
1 clove garlic, crushed
50 ml lemon juice
80 g blue vein cheese
Salt and pepper to taste

SALAD
1 ½ cups cooked chick peas
500 g roasted pumpkin pieces
¼ cup pumpkin seeds
½ cup red capsicum, diced
¼ cup red onion, finely sliced
2 cups baby chicory leaves
¼ cup chicory flower petals plus extra petals to garnish
¼ cup mint leaves

CANDIED PECANS: Heat the ingredients in a small frying pan over moderate heat until the sugar melts. Stir regularly to prevent burning. Turn the heat up a little if required and bubble the sugar 2 minutes to candy. Tip onto a biscuit tray lined with baking paper to cool.

DRESSING: Add all ingredients to a blender and whizz on high speed until the dressing is smooth. It keeps 3 days in the fridge.

SALAD: Add the salad ingredients to a bowl and toss to combine. Top with the dressing, candied pecans and extra chicory flower petals.

Cornflower
Centauria cyanus

GROWING: Cornflowers produce masses of fine foliage with flowers at the tips of the foliage. This annual is a native of the United Kingdom, but grows surprisingly well right through to the subtropics until the wet weather really sets in. The flower heads are a mass of blue petals that retain their colour even when dried.

Sow seed 1 cm deep directly into soft, fertile soil from autumn to spring. Keep the seed bed moist as the seed germinates. The foliage is delicate and fern-like. Seeds may also be sown into punnets then transferred when plants are at 3-4 leaf stage. They tend to suffer from powdery mildew if the weather is humid. Spray weekly with foliar applications of eco-seaweed to help strengthen the cell walls and ward off fungal attack.

HARVESTING AND EDIBLE PARTS:
The repeat harvesting of flowers promotes more blooms. Both the green sepals which look like tiny leaves behind each flower head and the white base of the petals are bitter. Cut them off when using or preserving these flowers.
To dry, dehydrate the petals and store in an airtight jar for use in breakfast granola, shortbread, herbal teas and chai tea mixes.

Cornflowers have been traditionally used as poultices for reducing inflammation in sore joints and in eye washes. They were once made into 'medicinal' wine to treat everything from vertigo to coughs.

COLOUR: Blue

SUN/SHADE: Full sun, part shade

PLANTING: Seed-autumn to winter depending on climate

FLOWERING: Early spring to Christmas

HEIGHT: About 75 cm

GROWER'S NOTE: It's a curious quirk of nature that cornflowers have very little fragrance when fresh, but become highly aromatic when crystallised.

Cornflower granola and coconut yoghurt cups

This recipe for granola is a favourite with our family. The dried petals are made by the flowerfetti method on page 8.

MAKES 6 CUPS GF, V, DF

1 cup chopped almonds
¾ cup raw cashews
½ cup sunflower seeds
¼ cup dried cornflower petals*
¾ cup activated buckwheat**
½ cup dried cranberries
1 cup quinoa flakes
1 cup grated carrot
½ cup grated apple
2 teaspoons orange zest
¾ cup orange juice
3 tablespoons honey
5 teaspoons mixed spice

COOK'S NOTES: *Or use 1 cup fresh cornflower petals if they are in season in your garden. **Activated buckwheat is made by soaking and draining the raw seeds several times a day over a couple of days, to the point of germination. The buckwheat is then drained and dehydrated. The result is a crisp seed. This process softens the seed and removes plant proteins that can cause gut irritation.

TO SERVE: Coconut yoghurt, seasonal fruits, edible flowers

Soak the almonds, cashews and sunflower seeds for 4 hours in filtered water to reduce tannins and phytic acid. Soaking seeds begins the germination process. Rinse and drain in a colander. Add remaining ingredients to a large bowl. Mix them together with your hands.

Spread the mixture over two dehydrator sheets and dehydrate on 42°C for 12 hours or until dried. If you don't have a dehydrator, spread the moist granola mix onto baking paper lined cake coolers. Put these on baking trays and sit them in a cool oven maximum 50°C. It will be ready in less time than a dehydrator, so check for dryness every hour or so.

When dry and crisp, crumble the granola. Allow to cool, then store in an airtight jar. It will keep a few weeks. If it becomes soft, simply pop back into the dehydrator or cool oven for 10 minutes to crisp up again.

Layer into glasses with coconut yoghurt, flowers and fruit for a nutritious breakfast.

Cosmos, Mexican Aster
Cosmos sulphureus, C. caudatus, C. bipinnatus

GROWING: *Cosmos sulphureus* are yellow and gold flowers on an open, somewhat straggly plant. *Cosmos. bipinnatus and C. caudatus* flower in shades of pink, purple and burgundy and tend to be leafier with softer green foliage. *Cosmos bipinnatus* has been extensively bred to produce a huge array of petal shapes and colours. A further species, *Cosmos atrosanguineus* is also called the chocolate cosmos as it has brown flowers but is probably inedible. All cosmos are thought to originate from volcanic soils in the Mexico region.

Cosmos are lovely annuals in cottage gardens. In our own garden, they're planted among the vegetables and orchard as they make wonderful companion plants, attracting predators and feeding bees.

Sow seed directly into fertile garden beds and protect them from snails and slugs as they grow. In cold areas, raise seed in seed trays before planting out. Dwarf varieties are very suited to pots.

HARVESTING AND EDIBLE PARTS: The large petals around the golden disc are the edible part. Leaves are bitter and unpalatable.

Cut flowers will last a few days in a vase of water and you can pluck the petals off as you need them. Petals of *C. bipinnatus* are recurved and can hide insects.

COLOUR: Yellow to burgundy depending on species

SUN/SHADE: Full sun, part shade

PLANTING: Seed-autumn to spring depending on climate

FLOWERING: All year in warm areas; spring and summer in cooler climates

HEIGHT: 50 cm-1.2m

GROWER'S NOTE: Remember to cut off dead flowers (called deadheading), to promote a longer flowering season. If you wish to keep seeds for next year, dry the flower heads in paper bags and separate the seeds off before storing.

Cosmos and strawberry frozen layer cake

This is a lovely chilled dessert. Make it up to a week before you need it and keep it in the freezer. Allow it to thaw and decorate with fresh flowers when ready to serve. If there are leftovers, refreeze without the flower decorations.

SERVES 8-10 GF, V, DF

CRUST
1 cup almonds, soaked 4 hours then drained
8 pitted soft dates
⅓ cup sunflower seeds soaked 4 hours
1 ½ tablespoons coconut oil
½ teaspoon salt

CASHEW LAYER
2 cups raw cashews, soaked 2 hours then drained
⅓ cup coconut oil
3 lemons zested and juiced
¼ cup coconut water
⅓ cup honey
1 teaspoon vanilla paste

STRAWBERRY LAYER
30 ml lime juice
30 ml water
8 g agar agar (Jell-It-In)
250 g fresh or frozen strawberries
1 cup cooked sweetened rosellas with ¼ cup juice*

COOK'S NOTE: *You may substitute cooked sweetened plums for rosellas.

TO SERVE: Fresh cosmos and herb flowers.

CRUST: Use a food processor to process all the ingredients to a fine crumb. Press the crumb mix into a parchment or foil-lined 20 cm springform pan. Chill.

CASHEW LAYER: Ensure all ingredients are at room temperature and that the coconut oil is liquid. Whizz the ingredients in a blender for 1 to 2 minutes until silky smooth. Pour the cashew mixture over the crust and freeze.

STRAWBERRY LAYER: Make this layer once the cashew layer is firm. Place the lime juice, water and agar in a saucepan. Mix until dissolved. Bring to the boil then turn off heat. Add the berries and rosellas to the saucepan and heat through gently until the agar is once again dissolved. Cool just a little. Blend the mixture until smooth.

Pour over the cashew layer and freeze. Serve thawed, topped with a garland of flowers.

Crucifix Orchid, Star Orchid
Epidendrum ibaguense

GROWING: These delightful orchids from Central and South America, are hailed as 'beginner' orchids as they are so easy to grow. They'll thrive in pots or in ground, in the warmest spot possible as frosts can kill them. Once established, they are drought tolerant. The old-fashioned orange flowered variety can be weedy in warm seaside areas, whereas the more modern hybrids are considered less so.

Crucifix Orchids are grown from aerial shoots called 'pups' or 'keikis', which form on a previously flowering stem. When the roots on the keiki are about 5-10 cm long, snip off the keiki and plant into an open moist soil with compost, coconut peat and Organic Xtra fertiliser. They love bright light and fail to flower well in deep shade.

These orchids require minimal care. Apply an organic fertiliser in summer and again early spring. Select a fertiliser high in potassium and low in nitrogen to stimulate flowers rather than leaves.

HARVESTING AND EDIBLE PARTS: The tiny crisp flowers that resemble coloured stars have a slightly oily flavour. I've tasted many colours. They are reported to each have their own flavour but they all taste the same to me. They transport well, they don't bruise and they store well in a covered container for over a week.

COLOUR: A range of colours including purple, pink, red, orange

SUN/SHADE: Full sun to bright shade

PLANTING: Plantlets-warm months

FLOWERING: Year-round with a big flowering burst in spring

HEIGHT: 1.2 m x 1 m wide

GROWER'S NOTE: Many orchid flowers are edible, but do not eat the artificially coloured blooms. Cymbidium Orchids are considered edible but contain alkaloids such as quinone which cause skin reactions in some people.

Crucifix Orchid sponge

This sponge cake is quick and easy. It will impress your guests with its flamboyance when decorated with the Crucifix Orchids. It's a traditional sponge cake, which is as light and lovely as you may remember from childhood, with a sensual attraction in all those blooms.

MAKES 1 DOUBLE LAYERED
SPONGE V

4 eggs, separated
¾ cup caster sugar
1 cup self raising flour, sifted
1 teaspoon cream of tartar
½ teaspoon bicarb soda
1 tablespoon custard powder
¾ cup cornflour
Pinch salt
400 ml pure cream
¼ cup lavender jelly page 152
or warmed berry jam
1 tablespoon floral syrup. Use
violet, rose, elderflower, or rosella.

TO SERVE: Crucifix Orchids, elderflowers, peppermint geranium leaves

Grease and line two 20 cm sponge tins with baking paper. Heat the oven to 180°C.

Beat the egg whites in a medium mixer bowl until stiff. Add the yolks and then the caster sugar and beat until the sugar is dissolved.

Sift the flour, cream of tartar, bicarb soda, custard powder, cornflour and salt into a bowl. Gently fold sifted ingredients into the egg mixture. Pour into sponge tins.

Bake in a moderate oven 30 minutes. When golden on top and spongy to touch, remove from the oven and cool on a cake rack for two minutes before turning out of the tins. Remove the backing the paper when you are ready to assemble the sponge cakes.

ASSEMBLY: Whip the cream and floral syrup together until firm peaks form. Place the first sponge cake onto a plate. Spread the jelly or jam over this one and top with half the cream. Add the next layer and spread with cream. Decorate with flowers and leaves.

Dahlia
Dahlia species

GROWING: Dahlias are grown from a large tuber that resembles a sweet potato. Plant the tubers into enriched, moist soil with a little sprinkle of wood ash. Insert a stake beside the tuber at the time of planting, as the stems on the taller growing varieties will need support. I've found one foliar application of liquid potassium fertiliser, as they come into flower, creates more vibrant flower colours.

The tubers can stay in the ground year-round, but most growers dig them up once the plant has died down in early winter. Store them in a cool dry spot until the first little buds appear in spring. It's then time to plant them again.

These gorgeous plants originate from the areas around Mexico and Colombia where both petals and tubers were used as food. The hollow stems were also used as drinking straws. While the original dahlias were very simple, we now have a plethora of sensational hybrids.

HARVESTING AND EDIBLE PARTS: To use the flowers, choose freshly opened blooms. Add them to salads and cake toppings. The flowers will keep in a vase of water for 2-3 days. The petals stay fresh a little longer when chilled. They also make a pretty flower confetti which is used in the recipe to follow.

Dahlia root is a source of inulin, as is the root of another edible South American plant, Yakon. Inulin derived from dahlias, was used to treat diabetics before the advent of insulin. Dahlia petals have been used in folk medicine for foot soaks and skin applications.

COLOUR: A range of pastel and bright colours

SUN/SHADE: Full sun

PLANTING: Tubers-spring

FLOWERING: Summer

HEIGHT: Up to 2 m

GROWER'S NOTE: Slugs and snails will devour your dahlia shoots as they emerge. Protect your dahlias from these voracious feeders by trapping with organic slug and snail traps loaded with potassium pellets such as Escar-go.

Raspberry and dahlia petal meringues

Our daughters loved meringues when they were little. The pinker the better! These meringues are certainly pink, coloured with fruits and flowers. Eat them on the day of making. They are delicate meringues which will collapse in humid conditions.

MAKES 8-10 LARGE
MERINGUES GF, V

4 egg whites (about 120 g in total)
250 g caster sugar
1 teaspoon white vinegar
1 tablespoon cornflour
⅓ cup frozen raspberries
Whipped cream and dahlia petal
flowerfetti* to serve.

COOK'S NOTE: *You'll find the instructions for creating the flowerfetti (dried petals) on page 8.

Heat oven to 120°C. Line two baking trays with baking paper. Beat the egg whites with an electric mixer until they make a soft peak. Add the sugar, vinegar and cornflour to the egg whites and beat again until firm peaks form.

Briefly blend or food process the frozen raspberries until they break up into segments. Use a spoon or spatula to gently fold raspberries through the egg whites, leaving lots of streaks. Just a few folding turns with your spatula should do the trick.

Place tablespoonfuls of meringue onto the lined baking trays and cook for 20 minutes. Turn the heat to 100°C and cook a further 30 minutes. Take care to keep the oven temperature low enough that they don't colour.

Remove from the oven and allow to cool a few minutes before using an egg slice to transfer them to biscuit trays. To serve: Top each meringue with whipped cream and sprinkle over the dried or fresh dahlia flowerfetti.

Daylily, Golden Needles
Hemerocallis species

GROWING: Daylilies are upright, strappy leaved, clumping plants. They are frost tolerant. Flower spikes (scapes) grow taller than the leaves in most cases and produce many buds per scape. Daylilies have been extensively bred and now thousands of cultivars, with magnificent flower colours, petal forms and sizes, are available. Daylily blooms only last 1 day, but there are usually many more to follow.

To grow them, plant root divisions (crowns) into a sunny spot with fertile soil. Mulch after planting. Apply potash as flowering commences. Foliar applications of a balanced organic fertiliser will encourage healthy plants.

Separate your daylilies every 2-3 years and replant the separated clumps after trimming the leaves. They can be grown from seeds, but seeds may not grow true to parent colour.

HARVESTING AND EDIBLE PARTS: Harvest the flowers and full, firm buds in the morning while still crisp. Buds can be refrigerated for a couple of days. Use the flowers the day you pick them. Before consumption, remove the central pistil and the stamens that bear the bitter pollen.

Daylily flowers have so many culinary uses. The buds are delicious as a savoury dish, sautéed with butter, tamari soy and a little chilli. Buds can be pickled in a sweet vinegar as for sweet pickled onions. For a dessert, caramelize the buds and serve with ice-cream. Heat butter and brown sugar until it bubbles. Add the buds and stir for 2 minutes before adding cinnamon and a squeeze of orange juice.

COLOUR: A range of colours including yellow, orange, white, reds

SUN/SHADE: Full sun

PLANTING: Divide and replant after flowering

FLOWERING: Spring and summer

HEIGHT: 30-90 cm

GROWER'S NOTE: Daylily Rust creates orange-red spots or blotches on the leaves. It's prevalent in humid weather. Treat rust organically using foliar sprays of eco-fungicide. Alternatively, casuarina leaf 'tea' can be used. Soak a big handful of casuarina leaves in 7 litres of hot water for 24 hours. Filter before spraying.

Mascarpone stuffed daylily flowers

Daylily flowers have many culinary uses. Most of the time I just nibble away at the crisp, slightly sweet petals while pottering in the vegetable patch. This recipe is for delectable, sweetly filled flowers. They are immensely popular at the Edible Flowers High Teas here at Ecobotanica.

SERVES 12 GF, V

12 daylily flowers
125 g mascarpone cheese
125 g cream cheese at room temp
¼ cup caster sugar
1 orange, zested
1 tablespoon lemon or orange liqueur*
1 cup pure cream whipped to soft peaks

COOK'S NOTE: *I make our own limoncello and orangecello when citrus are abundant. It's just lemon rinds infused into vodka for a month then strained out, with a sugar syrup added to the vodka. It's perfect for this recipe.

Remove the pollen-bearing stamens from the centre of the daylily flowers using small scissors.

Using an electric beater, beat the mascarpone with cream cheese, sugar, orange zest and liqueur. Fold in the whipped cream.

Spoon the mixture into a piping bag with a large star nozzle. Pipe the mixture into the centre of the daylily flowers. Serve as close to preparation time as possible.

These are delicious eaten as they are. Pick off the crispy petals and dip them into the mascarpone filling to enjoy a floral delight.

Dianthus, Pinks, Clove Pinks
Dianthus species

GROWING: Perennial and annual forms of dianthus are available. The perennial forms are fragrant and look like perfect miniature carnations. The annual or bedding dianthus are open and flat and usually without fragrance. Both forms are small, tufting plants.

Perennial dianthus, also called Pinks, have grey-green grass-like leaves and last many years in the garden. These can be successfully divided and transplanted. Just trim off some cuttings and settle into potting mix. Keep damp until they take root, then transplant into the garden or pots. Add one tablespoon of dolomite to the soil around each plant annually.

Annual dianthus have dark green soft leaves. Their multi-coloured flowers have a central 'eye' of colour and serrated petals. They are grown from pepper-fine seed in spring. Chill the seed two days before sowing.

Trim off old blooms to encourage new flowers.

HARVESTING AND EDIBLE PARTS: Harvest the flowers in the morning while they are still cool and fragrant and while the petals are firm. If you use the petals alone, trim them from the green sepals using scissors. Using the whole flower is perfectly fine.

COLOUR: A wide range of colours, except blue

SUN/SHADE: Full sun to part shade

PLANTING: Divisions-spring to summer; seed-spring, autumn in warm areas

FLOWERING: Spring to autumn

HEIGHT: Under 30 cm

GROWER'S NOTE: Dianthus, or Clove Pinks, with their wonderful clove scent are also called Gillyflowers or Sops. Historically, they were steeped in wine to make the drink 'Sops in Wine'. They are an ingredient in Chartreuse liqueur.

Dianthus flower pots with carob mousse

These are simple but spectacular and never cease to draw a gasp of wonderment from guests. The flower pots are filled with dairy-free, avocado mousse. The clove-flavoured dianthus complement the mousse.

MAKES ABOUT 6 SMALL POTS
GF, V, DF

3 ripe avocadoes
1 ripe banana, peeled
2 teaspoons organic vanilla paste
1 teaspoon ground cloves
⅓ cup carob powder
⅓ cup maple syrup or honey

COOK'S NOTE: Buy the tiny terracotta pots from nurseries. Wash well and put them into a cool oven, then heat to 150°C. Time 20 minutes once the temperature has been reached to sterilise them the first time.

TO SERVE: Dianthus flowers, petals, baby herb and vegetable leaves.

Scoop the avocado flesh, banana, vanilla paste cloves, carob and maple syrup or honey into a blender. Start the blender on the ice crushing setting to break up the avocado and banana pieces, then change to the 'high' speed setting to liquefy. Once it looks smooth and silky, turn off the blender. Have a little taste. It looks like chocolate mousse and tastes heavenly.

Pipe or spoon the mousse into the pots. Top with the flowers and leaves. Add a layer of leaves to the serving plate and place the pots on the plate to serve. This is dessert at its healthiest. You can eat the salad too if you like.

Elderflower
Sambucus nigra, S. racemosa, S. canadensis

GROWING: Umbrella-shaped heads of fragrant flowers abound in warmer months on this loose, open shrub. With age and pruning, elderflower can take the form of a small tree, or it may be kept pruned as a hedged shrub. I find it easier to prune low for harvest. Birds love the berries, so if you want to use them keep the plant low enough to net.

It's easy to grow if you give it regular moisture and fertiliser for abundant flowers. It grows so well from bird-dropped seed along stream banks, that it's often recognized as a pest species. Other species of Sambucus may be poisonous eg. *S. ebulus* so to be sure, just use those listed above.

Grow from suckers, cuttings taken in spring, or from seed. A warm wet spot is ideal. It will survive in a dry spot but not flower as profusely.

To sow seed, crush the berries and soak them in a cup of water. The seeds will float. Scoop the seeds off and sow in a compost or worm casting-enriched organic potting mix.

HARVESTING AND EDIBLE PARTS: Harvest the flowers when freshly opened, before they begin to turn colour. The flowers are edible but the stems and leaves should not be eaten. The black elderberries are also edible but ONLY when cooked.

Fritters anyone? You can make fabulous little fritters using the flower heads. Just dip the heads into a tempura batter, then fry in oil for 20 seconds until golden. Sprinkle with icing sugar and eat immediately. There's a video on how to make elderflower fritters at
www.ecobotanica.com.au/videos

COLOUR: White

SUN/SHADE: Full sun to bright shade

PLANTING: Plant suckers anytime; seed-spring

FLOWERING: Spring to summer

HEIGHT: 2-6 m

GROWER'S NOTE: BEWARE: The berries, leaves and stems contain cyanide-inducing glycosides that if consumed raw, will cause vomiting and stomach cramps.

Elderflower fizz

This traditional English elderflower 'fizz' or 'champagne' is always a hit. Make it in plastic bottles so you can monitor the expansion and avoid explosions. It's a little alcoholic, so not suitable for children.

MAKES 4.5L GF, V, DF

6 large heads of elderflower, shaken to remove any bugs
4.5 litres filtered water
2 lemons, sliced
750 g sugar
2 tablespoons cider vinegar
½ teaspoon champagne yeast from brewing stores*
Plastic fizzy drink bottles to hold the elderflower fizz.

COOK'S NOTES: *Champagne yeast is optional. It creates a fizzier and more alcoholic drink than relying on a natural airborne yeast to colonise your elderflower fizz.

I must admit a severe partiality to elderflower anything! I make champagne, syrup and cordial. A syrup made with lemons, sugar and fresh flower heads can be used as a flavouring in cakes, yoghurt, mixed drinks and ice-cream.

Select young flower heads when the flowers have just started to open. Heads with brown flowers are not suitable. Put the water into a large boiler saucepan with lid. Add the elderflower heads and lemons. Put the lid on and leave 36 hours.

Strain the liquid through a piece of clean muslin or cheesecloth into a large bowl or pan.

Add the sugar, vinegar and champagne yeast if using and stir to dissolve. Pour into bottles, leaving 4cm for expansion. Cap but don't screw the cap on tightly. You'll see the bubbles start to form over the next day or so. This indicates fermentation has started.

Depending upon the season, the bubbles slow down after about 1 week (It's slower in winter). At this stage, screw the lids on tightly. Keep a close eye on the bottles. If they seem too fat and extended, loosen the cap to release some bubbles. You don't want the bottle to burst.

Leave another 3-5 days before refrigerating. It keeps for weeks in the fridge. Serve full strength or with a little mineral water. The longer you keep it the less sweet it will be, as the yeasts use the sugar.

Fennel, Florence Fennel, Bronze and Green Fennels
Foeniculum vulgare

GROWING: Fennel is thought to originate from Greece. There is only one species of fennel with many subspecies. *Foeniculum vulgare* subspecies vulgare includes perennial fennels such as Green Fennel. Bronze Fennel is a cultivar 'Rubrum' while F. variety *azoricum* is the annual Florence Fennel.

Of all the fennels, I find the Florence Fennel with the fat white bulbs to be the most useful in my garden. In winter and spring we enjoy the licorice flavoured bulbs. In summer, as any extra plants go to flower and seed, I make use of the seeds too.

Fennel is easy to grow from seed. Soak the seeds for 2-3 days in water then sow seed into seedling trays. Cover with 1 cm soil and keep moist. Transplant to fertile soil 1 month later when the seedlings are about as tall as your middle finger. Space seedlings 20 cm apart.

Aphids love fennel. If you have an infestation, use eco-oil spray to kill them. Humid weather can also cause a white coating of powdery mildew on the leaves. To prevent this, a fortnightly foliar application of eco-seaweed will strengthen the leaves to ward off mildews.

HARVESTING AND EDIBLE PARTS: If you love the flavour of licorice and aniseed, then fennel is for you. Flower heads in the shape of an umbel (umbrella), are best harvested when open and bright yellow. Seeds can be eaten green or dried.

All above ground parts are edible. Florence Fennel forms a bulb. Pick the bulb by cutting off at ground level when it's firm and white. Harvest leaves at any time, cutting with sharp scissors.

COLOUR: Lemon yellow

SUN/SHADE: Full sun

PLANTING: Seed-winter to late spring depending on climate

FLOWERING: Spring and summer

HEIGHT: Up to 2 m

Fennel seed tea is recognized as an ingredient in colic medicines for babies. The oil has been used as a diuretic, analgesic and antifungal treatment.

GROWERS NOTE: Bronze Fennel tends to be weedy, so if you live in the country do the environment a favour and plant Green Fennel or Florence Fennel instead.

Almond beetroot spoons with fennel flowers

Fennel is often paired with seafood in recipes, but as a vegetarian I love it with almonds and root vegetables. It brings out their earthy characteristics. This recipe is a bite-sized starter. The fennel flowers are quite a surprise as they add a big buzz to each mouthful. Make the almond 'cheese' a day or two before.

SERVES 6 GF, V, DF

ALMOND 'CHEESE'
½ cup raw almonds
2 tablespoons water
1 dairy-free probiotic capsule
2 teaspoons lemon juice
Pinch salt
1 teaspoon fresh fennel leaves, snipped
2 teaspoons parsley, snipped

PICKLED BEETROOT
12 baby beetroots
350 ml sweet pickling vinegar

COOK'S NOTE: *Activating (soaking) almonds removes tannins that can affect digestion.

TO SERVE: Serving spoons, fresh fennel flowers and leaves

ALMOND 'CHEESE': Soak the raw almonds for two hours in filtered water then drain*.

Put the almonds, water, probiotic capsule, lemon juice and salt into a blender and blend until you have a fine-grained texture. Transfer to a bowl and stir in the herbs. Cover and sit in a warm spot 10-12 hours to culture. Refrigerate after culturing.

PICKLED BEETROOT: Peel the baby beets. Steam until they are just beginning to soften. Pack them into small warmed jars. Heat the vinegar to boiling point and allow to cool a little, so as not to break the jars. Pour the vinegar over the beets and seal. They are ready to use when cool. Store for a week in the fridge if necessary.

To serve, add a teaspoon of almond 'cheese' to each spoon. Top with a drained and dried baby pickled beetroot, a fennel flower and some leaves.

Ginger - Galangal Ginger, Kaa (Thai.)
Alpinia galangal

GROWING: Galangal Ginger varies from the culinary ginger we commonly use. The root is pink when fresh with a lemony, peppery flavour. It's evergreen in warm areas and does not need lifting every year. Just dig out a root and use it, leaving the clump standing.

Galangal Ginger needs warm, frost-free conditions and I recommend a soft, sandy soil for planting. Its roots are numerous and, when planted in a clay soil, it's challenging to harvest the root. Cut down the leaves every 2-3 years in winter and fertilise with an all-round fertiliser containing silica and potassium. Dig root pieces for transplanting at any time of the year.

Provide an application of Organic Xtra fertiliser in spring and again in summer and keep the soil moist.

HARVESTING AND EDIBLE PARTS: Galangal Ginger has a spike of flowers that open sequentially from the base. When harvesting, gently pick off the flowers and buds as they bruise easily. Store in a covered container in the fridge for one to two days. The pink rhizomatous roots, young shoots and flowers are edible. The oil from galangal ginger is used to flavour Angostura Bitters and Chartreuse. Roots will keep for weeks in the crisper of the fridge.

Edible ginger flowers usually taste similar to the roots of their corresponding plant species and the galangal flower is no exception. It has an intense peppery, lemon spice flavour which tingles on the tongue. A little goes a long way. The root and flower are used in curry pastes and soups. Flowers are sometimes ground into chilli paste for a condiment.

COLOUR: Cream

SUN/SHADE: Full sun to part shade

PLANTING: Plant rhizomes late summer to winter

FLOWERING: Mid to late summer

HEIGHT: 2-3m

GROWER'S NOTE: Allow plenty of space for your ginger clumps. They will expand width-ways with age and galangal grows tall.

Ginger flower dipping sauce

You'll trick your guests when you create a dish with these flowers as they probably won't be able to identify them. This dipping sauce is a peanut-based sauce that works beautifully with the floral spring rolls on page 40.

MAKES ABOUT 1 CUP GF, V, DF

½ cup smooth peanut butter
¼ cup warm water to mix
1 ½ tablespoons tamari soy sauce
1 teaspoon chilli powder or fresh chilli
2 tablespoons honey
50 ml lime juice
1 heaped tablespoon finely chopped ginger flowers eg galangal or torch ginger petals plus extra to sprinkle on top

Place the peanut butter in a small bowl with the water and mix well with the back of a spoon until combined.

Add the tamari soy sauce, chilli powder or finely chopped fresh chilli, honey and lime juice. Stir to mix. Finally, add the ginger flowers and stir through.

Serve in a small bowl with extra petals sprinkled on the top. It's perfect for dipping spring rolls into. This dipping sauce is also delicious with traditional Thai entrees, like Money Bags, and is even great over a green salad.

If you have peanut allergies, use an alternative nut butter such as almond or macadamia.

Ginger - Torch Ginger, Bunga Kantan (Mal.) Kaalaa (Thai.)
Etlingera elatior

GROWING: Not all gingers have edible flowers, but the Torch Ginger is both spectacular and delicious. This semi-deciduous plant is upright and clumping, thriving in a rich soil with plenty of summer water. The flowers are held upright on stalks about 1 metre tall.

Torch Ginger needs warm, frost-free conditions. Provide a space in the garden that will accommodate a 2 metre clump. Cut down the leaves in winter and fertilise the plant with an all-round fertiliser containing silica and potassium. If you wish to propagate your plant, dig up pieces and transplant in winter.

To grow from seed, soak ripe seeds overnight in water. Sow 2 cm deep in potting mix the following day. Keep warm and moist.

Once the weather warms, the clump springs to life. Provide compost, regular applications of organic fertiliser, plenty of water in summer but not too wet in winter. It may take Torch Gingers several years to flower profusely.

HARVESTING AND EDIBLE PARTS: Harvest Torch Ginger flowers in the morning when they are still fresh. Cut long stems with a pair of secateurs. Remove any old petals by cutting them off in a circular motion around the stem. The flowers last 3-5 days. Torch Ginger preparations have been used in folk medicine to treat ear infections, high blood pressure and diabetes. Stems, buds, flowers and the seeds that form after flowering are all edible.

COLOUR:	White through to red
SUN/SHADE:	Full sun to part shade
PLANTING:	Divide clumps and plant autumn to winter. Sow ripe seeds-summer
FLOWERING:	Spring to Summer
HEIGHT:	3-4 m

Torch Ginger salad with tempe and rice noodles

If you haven't tried eating Torch Ginger flowers before, you are in for a culinary delight. Check the ecobotanica.com.au website for an additional Torch Ginger recipe and a video on how to separate the petals. The fresh petals of the Torch Ginger add extra zing to this salad.

SERVES 6 V, DF

SALAD
3 cakes of rice vermicelli noodles
1 block of organic soy tempe
2 tablespoons Hoisin sauce
1 dessertspoon tamari soy sauce
1 tablespoon oil
¼ cup spring onions, sliced lengthways
1 cup green beans, blanched 1 minute in boiling water
1 cup bean sprouts
1 cup cherry tomatoes, quartered
2 tablespoons Vietnamese mint leaves, finely sliced

DRESSING
1 teaspoon grated ginger root
1 dessertspoon coconut vinegar
1 dessertspoon tamari soy sauce
2 tablespoons lime juice
1 teaspoon dulse (seaweed) flakes
1 teaspoon coconut palm sugar
A little sliced fresh chilli to taste

TO SERVE: Torch Ginger petals, a few sprigs of coriander; 2 tablespoons chopped salted peanuts.

To remove the Torch Ginger petals, pull off the large petals and grasp the flower stem in one hand, with the flower facing skywards. Using a sharp knife, cut around the base of the central flower bud to remove the bud. The petals are now easy to separate.

SALAD: Soak the rice vermicelli noodles in boiling water in a heat proof bowl until they are soft. Separate with chopsticks as they soften. Once soft, drain for use.

Cut the tempe into 1 cm cubes and coat in a mixture of the Hoisin sauce and tamari. Cook 2 minutes in a small frypan with the oil.

Combine the drained noodles, tempe and remaining salad ingredients in a serving bowl. Toss gently to combine. Sprinkle the Torch Ginger petals, coriander leaves and peanuts over the salad.

DRESSING: Combine all ingredients in a jar. Shake to dissolve the sugar and serve over the salad.

Jasmine Sambac, Arabian Jasmine, Sampaguita (Phil.)
Jasminum sambac

GROWING: The fragrant flowers of this evergreen open shrub release their perfume especially first thing in the morning or late in the evening. If you have an established plant, it's impossible to walk past without being enveloped in the scent.

Grow Jasmine Sambac in fertile soil with added manure. It may be propagated from cuttings in spring. Give it plenty of space to spread if you are not keen to prune often. I prune mine lightly each winter when it's partly deciduous.

Edible varieties, or 'sports' of the Jasmine Sambac include 'Maid of India', 'Belle of Orleans' and 'Grand Duke of Tuscany', which is a double form that resembles a tiny rose. This last one is my favourite for its flowers with a purple tinge. Each of the above varieties is suitable as an edible flower.

HARVESTING AND EDIBLE PARTS: Harvest the flowers in the early mornings or early evenings when the fragrance is at its headiest. Don't harvest leaves as they are not edible. I use scissors to trim off the petals from the green sepals.

Sambac Jasmine flavour many of our common dishes. Be aware though, that some jasmine flavourings may be oils or artificial flavours rather than from the flowers. There are several other jasmines touted for use as edible but I only use Jasmine Sambac. Some other jasmines will cause a burning sensation in the mouth if eaten.

I have fond memories of the fragrance from jasmine garlands wafting through the air in Thailand. They are used extensively in the tropics to make garlands for weddings and temple offerings and are the national flower of the Philippines.

COLOUR: White

SUN/SHADE: Full sun to part shade

PLANTING: Take cuttings in spring most areas, autumn-winter in tropics

FLOWERING: Spring to Summer

HEIGHT: 1-3m x 3m wide

GROWERS NOTE: Jasmine Sambac flowers are used for flavouring rice, jasmine tea and for perfumery.

Jasmine-scented custard tartlets

These jasmine tartlets are delicately scented, just like the flowers. If you are a keen pastry cook, make your own sweet short-crust pastry shells rather than using purchased tart shells.

MAKES 12 TARTLETS V

1 dozen pre-cooked, mini, sweet
short crust tartlet shells
425 ml full cream milk
¼ cup fresh or dried Sambac
Jasmine flowers
1 teaspoon orange zest
¼ cup caster sugar
1 ½ tablespoons custard powder
1 ½ tablespoons cornflour
2 tablespoons orange juice
50 ml pure cream

COOK'S NOTE: I make our own
jasmine-flavoured herbal tisane
(tea) using fresh or dried flowers

TO SERVE: Fresh Jasmine Sambac flowers.

Pour the milk into a saucepan and add the jasmine flowers and orange zest. Bring to a gentle simmer. Simmer 1 minute then remove from heat and steep 3 minutes. Strain the milk through a sieve into a bowl and return to the saucepan. Discard the jasmine flowers. Add sugar to the milk and gently warm to dissolve the sugar, stirring all the time.

Mix the custard powder and cornflour in a cup with a little water. As you stir the milk, pour the custard powder into the milk to incorporate. It will thicken quickly. Bring to a gentle bubble, stirring the custard continually for 1 minute to thicken. Take from the heat and stir through the orange juice. Pour the custard into a bowl and allow to cool to room temperature. When cool, pour in the cream and beat 1 minute with electric beaters.

Spoon into tartlet shells and top with flowers.

Lavender
Lavandula species

GROWING: Lavender is a much-loved perennial that cottage gardeners love to grow. While it flourishes in cooler, or Mediterranean climates, it can be a challenge in humid summers.

English or True Lavender, *L. angustifolia*, is most delicious for cooking but this plant enjoys dry summers and cool winters. For humid climes, try *L. allardii* and *L. stoechas* (with two little bunny ear petals on each spike). They have a more 'camphorous' flavour as the camphor oil levels are higher than the true lavender. *L. dentata* is not as suited to culinary purposes because the flowers are not as fragrant and easy to separate as English Lavender. Each species grows and flowers at a slightly different time of the year.

Grow from seed or take semi-hardwood cuttings in spring. Sometimes a branch will aerial layer, creating its own roots in the soil. This is a perfect start for you to trim it off, lift it and transplant.

Prepare your soil by ensuring a pH 6.5-8. Add a tablespoon of lime or dolomite to the soil around each plant annually, plus seasonal feeds of an all-purpose fertiliser, such as Organic Xtra fertiliser. Trim away low-hanging foliage to increase air circulation during humid summers. Trim flowers regularly and use hedge clippers to shape the bush. While drought tolerant, lavender grows better in moist, well drained soils and hates wet feet.

HARVESTING AND EDIBLE PARTS: You'll get the best results if you harvest the flowers while fresh and colourful. Gather small bundles of them together and tie with string. Hang the bundles in an airy room to dry, out of the sun so they retain their colour. Once dry, strip the flowers from the spikes and store in sealed jars. The lavender flowers mentioned above may be used for cooking either fresh or dried.

COLOUR: Lavender, pink or white

SUN/SHADE: Full sun

PLANTING: Sow seed or take cuttings spring to early summer most areas

FLOWERING: Spring and summer

HEIGHT: 1 m x 75 cm

GROWER'S NOTE: The most fragrant lavender for crafts is *Lavandula intermedia*.

Lavender shortcake with lavender jelly

Use fresh or dried lavender to flavour this decadent shortcake. The basic shortcake recipe was my mum's and I'm happy to give it a new lease of life. The lavender jelly is delicious with this shortcake, but if you don't have it in stock, use apricot jam instead. It will be nice, but not so wonderful!

SERVES 8-10 V

CUSTARD CREAM
100 ml milk
80 g custard powder
800 ml milk extra
½ cup caster sugar
1 teaspoon vanilla paste or essence
2 egg yolks

SHORTCAKE
250 g butter
1 cup caster sugar
2 large eggs
1 ½ cups self raising flour
1 ½ cups plain flour
1 ¾ cups milk
1 teaspoons dried lavender flowers (no stems)
Pinch salt
80 ml orange juice
80 ml purchased elderflower cordial
½ cup lavender jelly see page 152

TO SERVE: Lavender flowers, 1 sliced peach or other soft fruit, tiny meringues and chocolate leaves.

Heat oven to 190°C. Grease and line three 20 cm sponge tins with baking paper. Custard cream: Make the custard cream first so it can be chilling while the cake cooks. Add 100 ml milk to a bowl with the custard powder and blend.

Heat the remaining 800 ml milk, sugar and vanilla in a saucepan to bubbling point. Take off the heat and whisk in the egg yolks then custard powder mixture. Put back on the heat and stir constantly until the mixture thickens and boils for 1 minute. Cool then chill.

SHORTCAKE: Beat butter and sugar until creamy. Add the eggs and beat until just combined. Fold through the sifted flours, lavender flowers and salt, alternating with the milk. Spread the mixture equally between the sponge cake tins.

Bake 35 minutes or until pale golden and firm. Cool the cakes in the tins a few minutes before up-ending them to cool on the racks.

ASSEMBLY: Peel the paper from the cakes. Mix orange juice and elderflower cordial and drizzle one third over each cake. Spread two of the shortcakes with lavender jelly. Place the bottom one on a serving plate. Spread over 1/3 of the custard cream. Top with the next cake and layer with 1/3 custard cream. Add the top layer and the last of the custard cream Decorate with lavender flowers, (I've also added forget-me-nots), tiny lavender meringues, fruit and chocolate leaves.

Radish flowers
Raphanus sativus

GROWING: Radish are among the quickest seeds to germinate. The peppery roots can be harvested from five weeks after sowing the seed. Flowers take about three months to appear as the plant must go through maturation when the root will become quite large. You'll find a lovely range of heirloom radishes such as 'Watermelon', 'French Breakfast' and 'White Icicle', from Green Harvest Organic Seeds.

To plant radish, create a soft, compost enriched soil. Create rows 20 cm apart. Sow seeds 1 cm deep and a few centimetres apart for easy harvest. Avoid buying punnets of radish seedlings as root crops don't transplant well. After your seeds germinate, keep the plants moist for dense, sweet roots and lots of flowers.

Allow the radish to go to flower to provide you with plenty of delightfully peppery flowers. Collect seed for your next crop.

Bees, especially native stingless bees, love these flowers. You'll find them on the flowers, dusting themselves with pollen and nectar.

HARVESTING AND EDIBLE PARTS: The flowers are mild with a savoury crispness. The young leaves are peppery and hot and the fresh new seed pods that are shaped like little tadpoles are also tasty. Harvest in the cool of the day. The flowers keep well if refrigerated for several days.

Chefs are using radish flowers for canapès because they impart a delicate savoury pepperiness. The flowers are tiny and delicate. I have supplied some of Brisbane's most notable restaurants with these little flowers. I use them for savoury dishes and especially for garnishes when a small flower is called for.

COLOUR: White, or lavender depending upon the variety

SUN/SHADE: Full sun

PLANTING: Seed-any time

FLOWERING: Year-round except the coolest areas

HEIGHT: Flowers on tall stems up to 1 m

GROWER'S NOTE: Keep your seeds to sow in a cool, dark spot clear of insects. I recommend a sealable box in the coolest room in the house. This way, your seeds will remain viable for much longer.

Radish flower gazpacho soup with herbed sour cream

This chilled soup is outstanding as a refreshing summer starter. It has been a firm family favourite for decades. Our heirloom radishes flower white and purple, so the colour is lovely too. It takes only a few minutes to prepare.

SERVES 5 GF, V

HERBED SOUR CREAM
300 ml softly whipped sour cream
or stirred and softened crème
fraiche
3 tablespoons each of snipped
chives, basil and mint
2 tablespoons radish flowers
Ice cubes to serve

SOUP
1 cup tomato juice
2 ripe, soft tomatoes, quartered
1 small Lebanese or telephone
cucumber, cut into pieces
½ small green capsicum, cut
roughly
1 spring onion
1 tablespoon olive oil
1 tablespoon cider vinegar
1 clove garlic
¼ cup radish flowers, plus extra
to serve
8 ice cubes

HERBED SOUR CREAM: Mix the sour cream with the snipped herbs in a small bowl. Set aside. Keep the flowers to add to the top when serving.

SOUP: Divide the ingredients into two equal batches so your blender doesn't overflow. Blend the first batch until smooth, then pour into a jug. Repeat with the second batch.

Put a couple of ice cubes into each bowl or serving glass. Pour over the soup. Pipe on the herbed sour cream and sprinkle the radish flowers on the top. Serve immediately.

Store any leftover soup in the fridge for 24 hours. Stir well or blend briefly once again before serving.

Rose
Rosa species

GROWING: Roses are one of the world's most popular flowering plants. All organically grown roses are suitable for culinary use. The old garden roses, such as the Damask Roses, China Roses and Tea Roses are among the most heavily fragrant and make intensely flavoured recipes.

Take rose cuttings in spring as you prune them. Dip semi-hardwood cuttings into striking powder then push a few cuttings into each pot of cutting or potting mix. Keep moist until they form roots and new leaves.

Once cuttings have established, gently separate out the new plants that have formed and plant individually. Plant roses into fertile soil with aged cow manure and compost. To minimise fungal disease, allow plenty of space between plants for good airflow. Fortnightly eco-seaweed foliar sprays help to prevent fungal disease. Organic potassium bicarbonate spray, called eco-fungicide is effective in treating black spot. Aphids and scale are pests on roses too. Eco-oil will treat both these problems.

HARVESTING AND EDIBLE PARTS: Harvest roses in the morning while the petals are still firm. Cut blooms with a long stem to encourage a bushy plant. Rose petals are used extensively in a range of culinary delights. I've made rose flavoured Turkish delight, jam, sorbet, cakes and flavoured sugar. You may also use fresh petals in wine or jelly, or crystallised petals on cakes. Rose petal champagne sorbet is beautiful too. Find the recipe on page 150.

COLOUR: All except true blue

SUN/SHADE: Full sun to part shade

PLANTING: Cuttings-autumn to spring depending on climate

FLOWERING: Flushes of flower spring to autumn

HEIGHT: Depends on type

GROWER'S NOTE: My favourite heat tolerant roses include: 'Souvenir de la Malmaison' - small bush, pale pink, fragrant; 'Radox Bouquet' - bush, pink and sensually fragrant; 'Lorraine Lee' - bush/climber, apricot pink, fragrant; 'Mr Lincoln' - bush, dark red, fragrant and velvety; 'Ali Baba' – climbing, apricot, highly fragrant, repeat blooming; 'Climbing Pinkie' - miniature perfect pink buds, low fragrance.

Turkish delight ice cream

This ice cream is so simple yet fabulous. You must make it if you are a Turkish delight fan.
It's miles more fragrant and authentically flavoured than any you might buy in the shops, as
it has real flavour from the roses.

SERVES 10-12 V

3 cubes pink cornflour-coated
Turkish delight*
1 litre good quality vanilla ice
cream
1 teaspoon rose water
¼ cup pistachio nuts, chopped
¼ cup fragrant fresh rose petals
or 1 tablespoon rose petal
flowerfetti from page 8

COOK'S NOTE: *You may also
use chocolate covered Turkish
delight but the chocolate tends to
overpower this ice cream.

TO SERVE: Fresh rose petals and a floral ice bowl
(directions on page 10).

Chop the pink Turkish delight into tiny pieces, using a knife
dipped in icing sugar to stop it sticking. You may have to
roll the cut edges into the icing sugar as well. (Use soft icing
sugar mixture as the cornflour in it works more effectively to
stop the Turkish delight pieces from sticking.)

Take the ice cream from the freezer and spoon it into a
chilled bowl to soften a little. Using a large metal spoon, stir
the rosewater, pistachios and Turkish delight pieces into the
ice cream. You don't need to stir much, just a little to swirl it
through. Add the rose petals and gently stir a couple more
times to distribute the petals.

Pop the bowl into the freezer until serving time. Cover it to
prevent ice crystals forming.

To serve, scoop into a floral ice bowl and sprinkle over extra
rose petals.

Rosella, Roselle
Hibiscus sabdariffa

GROWING: Rosellas are tolerant of dry conditions, originating from tropical areas in Western Africa. They thrive in frost-free, subtropical and tropical areas with summer rainfall. Treat rosellas as annual plants, sowing seed each spring for a summer harvest.

Plant seed directly into fertile, composted soil. Sow into pots in cool areas to give them a head start. Sow in late spring in subtropical areas and earlier in hotter regions. The seeds require warm soil 25°C to germinate. As they grow, prune the branch tips lightly once or twice to ensure compact growth. Allow 12-15 weeks from planting to the start of flowering. They are a day length sensitive plant, so they flower as the days grow shorter.

Rosellas have a bright red, crisp calyx. This is the part that looks like rigid petals around the base of the flower. We grow rosellas each summer and they thrive in the heat. Treat them as an annual and pull them up after harvesting. You have the garden bed to grow a winter and spring crop before thinking about planting rosellas again for next season.

HARVESTING AND EDIBLE PARTS: Young leaves and flower petals are edible. It's the flowers and especially the red crisp calyces that develop after flowering, that I love. Harvest the calyces when firm and plump but not too woody. You will have many harvests over the growing period.

Rosellas are made into drinks, soups, pickles, jams and syrups. The seeds are rich in pectin which assists jam setting. Their use as dried pieces in herbal infusions is widespread. You know you are in Queensland when someone serves up rosella jam on scones. Rosellas are versatile in cooking. You can substitute cooked rosellas for blueberries or cranberries.

COLOUR: Lemon yellow to pale salmon

SUN/SHADE: Full sun

PLANTING: Seed-spring most areas

FLOWERING: Summer to autumn

HEIGHT: 1-2 m x 1 m wide

GROWERS NOTE: Watch a video on the Ecobotanica website **www.ecobotanica.com.au/videos** showing you how to harvest rosellas.

Rosella and white chocolate
cheesecake slice

When I developed this recipe years ago, our young neighbor Emma couldn't get enough of it. She popped in after school for days until it was all gone. It's rich but so deliciously smooth and delectable with the tang of rosellas.

SERVES 8-10 V

BASE
125 g unsalted butter, melted
250 g packet Butternut Snap biscuits, crushed finely in a blender or processor

CHEESECAKE
1 cup rosella preserves*
250 ml pure cream
150 g white chocolate
375 g cream cheese
¼ cup caster sugar
20 ml lemon juice
8 g agar agar (Jell-It-In)
1/3 cup water

COOK'S NOTE: *To make rosella preserves, separate the sepals and tepals (calyces) from the seed. Discard the seed and cook them in a light sugar syrup of 1 part sugar, 3 parts water. Bottle for use later in the year.

BASE: Line a 20 x 30 cm lamington tray with baking paper. Melt the butter in a medium sized saucepan. Tip in the crushed biscuits and mix well. Press the crumb mix into the prepared tin using the back of a metal spoon. Pop into the fridge to set firm.

CHEESECAKE: Drain the rosellas of most of their juice, retaining only one dessertspoon of juice. Whip cream to soft peaks. Melt the chocolate in a bowl over hot water.

Put the cream cheese, sugar and lemon juice into a medium bowl of an electric mixer and beat until combined and smooth. Fold through the whipped cream. Set aside.

Blend the agar and water in a small pan and heat to boiling point. Boil 30 seconds, stirring all the time. Allow to cool but not set. Pour it into the cream and cheese mixture, incorporating thoroughly. Fold through the melted chocolate then pour into the prepared biscuit base.

Finally, drop spoonfuls of rosella preserves onto the cheesecake. Using a knife, swirl the rosella preserves through the top of the cheesecake. Chill about 2 hours before serving.

Sesbiana, Agati, Hummingbird Flower
Sesbiana grandiflora

GROWING: Sesbiana is an open, branching tree or shrub that grows very fast in a warm spot with moist soil. It tolerates poor and saline soils and is a partly deciduous tropical plant. As it's a legume, it contributes significant nitrogen to the soil through its nitrogen-fixing nodular roots. Sesbiana will not tolerate cold, so it's only for the subtropics and warmer regions.

Grow it from seed in forestry tubes (which allow for a bigger root zone). They transplant well into the garden. Plant into a sheltered spot, as the Sesbiana timber is brittle and may be broken by high wind. Grow leafy greens under the tree such as lettuce, silverbeet and parsley, to take advantage of the free nitrogen.

Expect flowers after the first year of growth. It's the luck of the draw in Australia as to whether you get seeds of an early flowering (early summer) or late flowering (late summer) variety. Red flowered *Sesbiana grandiflora* are also available. By all accounts the red flowers are not so delicious. Prune the long branches after flowering to keep the tree compact and easily harvestable.

HARVESTING AND EDIBLE PARTS: Young leaves, seeds, pods and flowers are edible. Take care not to grow it near a pond, stream or dam, as the seeds are toxic to fish.

The flowers can be incorporated into salads, patties, used in curries and soups and deep fried. People from many tropical cultures consume Sesbiana (Hummingbird) flower and you'll see why when you taste the soup on the following page. They are crunchy and lovely. The flowers store well for at least 5 days in the fridge.

COLOUR:	White. Some have red flowers
SUN/SHADE:	Full sun
PLANTING:	Sow seed winter to spring
FLOWERING:	Spring and summer
HEIGHT:	Up to 15 m if untrimmed

Hummingbird Flower sour soup

The ingredient list for this sensational soup was shared with me by Julie, from Scrumptious Reads, a specialty bookshop in Brisbane. It's a richly flavoured, Asian-style broth, with a combination of seasonal vegetables and flowers. It was so popular in our family, that I made it three times in the first week.

SERVES 4-6, GF, V, DF

2 cups Hummingbird (Agati) flowers, cleaned
1 litre vegetable stock*
1 white stem of lemon grass
2 slices fresh ginger
3 kaffir lime leaves
3 Roma tomatoes, cut into wedges
1 dessertspoon coconut sugar
Chilli to taste
1 teaspoon tamarind puree
5 button mushrooms, sliced
2 spring onions, sliced finely
½ cup fresh corn kernels
150 g silken tofu, cubed (optional)

COOK'S NOTE: *For this recipe, I used Massel vegetable stock powder, 1 teaspoon per 250 ml.

TO SERVE: Extra Hummingbird flowers, squeeze lemon juice.

To clean the flowers, remove and discard the pollen-bearing parts from the flowers as they are bitter.

Pour the vegetable stock into a saucepan and add the pounded white stem of lemon grass, ginger slices, kaffir lime leaves, tomatoes, coconut sugar, chilli, tamarind puree and sliced button mushrooms.

Bring to a simmer then add the sliced spring onions, corn and Hummingbird flowers. Heat through then serve.

To serve, place a few cubes of silken tofu in each bowl. Ladle over the hot soup, ensuring you have cooked flowers in each bowl. Decorate with 2 or 3 fresh flowers. Squeeze a little lemon juice into each bowl and it's ready to enjoy.

Snapdragon, Dragon Flower
Antirrhinum majus

GROWING: Snapdragons are annuals that originated in China. They are easily grown from seed or seedling. I love to grow these 'snaps' as they appeal to my inner child with their little opening 'mouth'. In warm areas, they often flower well into the summer after spring planting, as they are quite tolerant of heat and humidity. Grow from seed in trays, then transplant into the garden, or grow from seedlings.

Before planting seed or seedlings, ensure the soil is fertile, enriched with humates and plenty of manure-based fertilisers. A fortnightly foliar application of liquid fertiliser will encourage flowering and healthy growth. If you are in a hot area, grow them in a lightly shaded garden bed or pot for a longer display.

Snapdragons make a beautiful bedding display as a mid-height grower, although dwarf forms are available. They grace our labyrinth garden in spring and summer with the spires of flowers. They are successful grown in pots or troughs too.

HARVESTING AND EDIBLE PARTS: Harvest the youngest flowers on the long spikes. They form as the spike grows, so you'll find the oldest flowers near the bottom of the spike and the youngest flowers towards the top. Open the little lip or lower petal of the flower before you use it, as sometimes an insect could be hiding there.

COLOUR: A range of colours except blue

SUN/SHADE: Full sun, part shade

PLANTING: Sow seed spring to summer in cool areas

FLOWERING: Spring and summer

HEIGHT: 30 cm

Snapdragon muffins with buttercream frosting

Muffins keep well for lunchboxes and morning teas and are simple to make. The snapdragon flowers chopped into the mix add texture to the muffins. Pull the green end from each flower before use. The buttercream frosting is coloured with natural Hopper's Colours (see cook's note) and fresh snapdragons.

MAKES 12-18 MUFFINS
DEPENDING UPON CUP SIZE
V

MUFFINS
2 ½ cups self raising flour
1 teaspoon bicarb soda
¾ cup sugar
⅔ cup mildly flavoured oil
eg sunflower
2 eggs
1 cup blueberries, mashed
½ banana, mashed
⅔ cup dairy or coconut yoghurt
¼ cup finely chopped snapdragon
flowers

BUTTER CREAM FROSTING
200 g butter at room temperature
1 teaspoon vanilla essence
2 ½ cups pure icing sugar
1 teaspoon lemon or lime juice
1-2 drops natural pink colouring
eg Hoppers colours

COOK'S NOTE: Hopper's
Colours are all natural, made
from vegetables and fruits.
They're available from health
food stores.

Heat the oven to 170°C

TO SERVE: Extra snapdragon flowers and tiny forget-me-nots.

MUFFINS: Add all the ingredients to a large mixing bowl and stir through with a spoon until combined. Don't beat it or the texture will become rubbery. Spoon the mixture into small to medium sized muffins tins, lined with paper cases.

Bake 20-25 minutes until firm and golden. Allow them to cool for 1 minute before tipping them onto a biscuit rack to cool.

BUTTER CREAM: Beat the butter and vanilla until pale in colour. Gradually add the icing sugar and continue to beat. Stir through the lemon juice. Divide the butter cream into two portions. Colour one portion only with the natural colouring. The second will stay the original colour. Spoon some of each colour butter cream into a piping bag with nozzle. Pipe onto each muffin and add a snapdragon to serve.

Society Garlic, Wild Garlic
Tulbaghia violacea

GROWING: Once relegated to ornamental gardens only, this aromatic clumping herb will provide you with abundant pretty flowers and mildly garlic flavoured leaves. They are either plain green or variegated-leaf plants. The variegated plants are not as vigorous and are a few centimetres shorter than their green counterparts. The garlic-flavoured flowers are held above the leaves on tall, stiff stems, like floral sparklers.

They are related to chives and garlic but are much more forgiving of difficult soil, extremes of heat and summer rain. Society Garlic flowers bloom for 8 months of the year.

To grow them, divide up clumps and plant a small clump into fertile soil, keeping it moist until new growth appears. A row of plants about 50 cm apart make a lovely border or entry feature to herb or vegetable gardens. Clumps expand quickly. I plant them under roses for their aphid-repelling properties. Trim off the flower stalks when dry.

HARVESTING AND EDIBLE PARTS: Harvest the flowers in the mornings when fully open. I remove the open flowers from the tall heads, allowing each head to produce more flowers over the coming days. The plain green Society Garlic has the darker flowers.

They are perfectly suited to savoury dishes as they give a hint of garlic. Mix into butters or cream cheese, use as a garnish on soups, in salads and finger foods. Leaves and white bulbous stems are also garlic flavoured.

COLOUR:	Mauve
SUN/SHADE:	Full sun to part shade
PLANTING:	From divided clumps any time in warm areas
FLOWERING:	Spring to autumn
HEIGHT:	30-40 cm

Society Garlic and pumpkin seed biscuits

These raw, gluten free biscuits are not cooked at high temperatures, but are dehydrated instead to retain flavour and nutrients. I've added the directions for preparing in both a dehydrator and oven. These biscuits freeze well once made too.

MAKES 1 TRAY OF BISCUITS
GF, V, DF

⅓ cup sundried tomatoes
¼ cup warm water
1 ½ cups pepitas
(pumpkin seeds)
½ cup pecans
½ cup golden flax meal
½ cup pitted black olives
1 teaspoon oregano leaves
1 teaspoon thyme leaves
1 tablespoon Society Garlic
leaves, snipped
¼ cup Society Garlic flowers
Salt and pepper

COOK'S NOTES: If they go soft, just pop them back into the dehydrator or oven a few minutes.

TO SERVE: Spread the biscuits with the calendula cheese on page 56 or the dairy free almond cheese on page 96. Decorate with edible petals, flowers and herbs

Soak the sundried tomatoes for 10 minutes in ¼ cup warm water. Drain and keep the soaking water as you'll be using it later. Chop the tomatoes with kitchen scissors.

Put the pepitas and pecans into a food processor. Process until you have fine crumbs. Add flax meal, chopped sundried tomatoes and the soak water, olives, oregano, thyme and Society Garlic leaves and flowers, salt and pepper to taste. Process on low speed until the herbs are combined and the mix is sticky.

Spread onto a dehydrator tray or biscuit tray lined with a non-stick sheet or parchment. Mark into squares. Dehydrate at 40°C for 4 hours, or 2 hours in an oven on its lowest temperature setting.

Flip the whole sheet of biscuits over and dehydrate a further 6-8 hours (about 2 hours in the oven) until crisp. Remove from the tray and break into pieces. Store in an airtight container in the pantry or freezer.

Sunflower
Helianthus annuus

GROWING: Sunflowers are an upright annual, originating in South America. Each plant bears one or more flowers on a central stem. Give them full sun and they will flourish, turning their ray-shaped flower heads to the sun.

Sow seed in fertile soil 40 cm apart, or in large tubs with premium organic potting mix. They flower 80-120 days after sowing, so plan your floral display in advance. As they grow, ensure continual soil moisture and apply fortnightly foliar feeds for magnificent blooms.

Giant Russian Sunflowers will grow at least 2-3 metres tall, so they may need staking in windy areas. The 'Evening Sun' range flower orange, pink, rust, burgundy and gold. For small spots and pots, dwarf sunflowers will also give you plenty of blooms.

Wild birds love sunflowers, so protect them from the cockatoos for example, who will demolish the flowers as the seeds are developing.

HARVESTING AND EDIBLE PARTS: You may want to pull off only the petals you need as I've found some sunflowers will form additional petals. Harvest the petals or whole flowers with long stems. The flowers keep well in a vase of water for three days.

Sunflower are best known in culinary circles for their seeds and oil, however the petals are lovely to use as a floral garnish. Petals dry well too. Strip them from the flower head before drying.

COLOUR:	Yellow, gold, bronze, pinks etc
SUN/SHADE:	Full sun
PLANTING:	Spring to autumn in warm areas
FLOWERING:	Spring to autumn
HEIGHT:	50 cm to 3 m depending on variety

GROWER'S NOTE: Grey striped seeds make for the best eating while black seeds are best for sunflower oil production.

Sunflower and basil pesto

We use this delicious pesto on biscuits, as a dip and on spiralised zucchini noodles, as a sauce. Just add a little more oil and water to the mix for a softer consistency when using it for sauce. It keeps for 5 days in the fridge, covered with a film of olive oil to prevent browning.

MAKES 1 ½ CUPS PESTO GF, V

3 cups basil leaves, lightly packed
¾ cup raw sunflower seeds
¼ cup raw pistachio nuts
¼ cup extra virgin olive oil
¾ cup grated parmesan cheese
2 cloves garlic, crushed
30 ml lemon juice
¼ cup water
Salt and pepper to taste
¼ cup sunflower petals, snipped

COOK'S NOTE: Sunflower petals can be added to any recipe that calls for sunflower seeds eg. sunflower seed bread. They take up very little 'room' in the recipe but add golden colour and look great raw or cooked. They are also commonly used as a garnish on salads.

TO SERVE: Fresh sunflower petals, Society Garlic and pumpkin seed biscuits page 136.

Wash and strip the basil leaves from the stems. Put the basil leaves, sunflower seeds, pistachios, olive oil, parmesan, garlic and lemon juice into a food processor. Process on medium speed until the nuts are roughly ground.

Add the water gradually through the chute to make a thick paste. Turn the paste (pesto) into a bowl and mix in salt and pepper to taste. Stir through the snipped sunflower petals.

Garnish the pesto with extra sunflower petals and a little oil. A thin layer of oil will stop the dip darkening off. Serve with Society Garlic biscuits.

Violets and Violas
Viola species

GROWING: Johnny Jump Ups, Heartsease Violas, Violets and Native Violets are all closely related plants in the genus Viola. They are annual plants except for the traditional fragrant purple violet, *Viola odorata* and the purple and white Australian Native Violet, *Viola hederacea*. These are both evergreen ground covers that quickly take over moist, fertile gardens.

Viola odorata flowers in spring and makes wonderful flavoured syrups. It needs a cool position. *V. hederacea* is not fragrant and loves a warm, part-shade position. Grow both from rooted parts of plants. Their creeping habit makes propagation easy.

Violas and pansies are annuals and grow well in many regions particularly over the cooler months. My favourites, the tiny Johnny Jump Ups, *Viola tricolor*, with purple, yellow and white flowers, are the most heat tolerant. They flower for much of the year. Pansies are hybridised forms of violas with larger flowers.

Viola plants typically stretch from compact plants into long sparse ones as the weather warms. If you are in a warm area search out the 'non-stretching' hybrids. Grow in spring, autumn and winter from seed sown directly into the garden bed or into pots or trays.

HARVESTING AND EDIBLE PARTS: Harvest the new, brightly coloured flowers with long stems. The regular removal of flowers helps to stimulate the plant to produce even more. Violas and violets are a delight to use in so many dishes. They are gorgeous frozen into ice blocks and make wonderful crystallised flowers. I add them to yoghurt, fruit salads and cake tops.

COLOUR: Range of colours including purple, yellow and white

SUN/SHADE: Full sun to shade

PLANTING: Seed-late summer to spring depending on area

FLOWERING: Winter to summer

HEIGHT: 15 cm x 40 cm wide

Lemon Myrtle panna cotta with crystallised Native Violets

This simple recipe for one of my favourite desserts, panna cotta, uses Native Violets as a beautiful garnish. You can also use fragrant violets, violas, pansies or Heartsease Violas. I use agar agar instead of gelatin to make it vegetarian.

MAKES 8 X 115 ML SERVES
GF, V

7 g agar agar (Jell-It-In)
⅓ cup water
300 ml pure cream
600 ml full cream milk
¾ cup white sugar
1 teaspoon vanilla bean paste
6 large Lemon Myrtle leaves fresh or dried

COOK'S NOTE: The directions for flower crystallisation is on page 8. Prepare the flowers up to a week in advance.

TO SERVE: Crystallised or fresh violets or violas

Add the agar and water to a saucepan. Stir to dissolve the agar, then turn on the heat to simmer for 30 seconds. Add the cream, milk, sugar and vanilla bean paste to the agar mixture. Heat once again until it begins to boil. Remove from the heat.

Put the Lemon Myrtle leaves into the milk mixture. Steep five minutes only then strain the milk to remove the leaves. Pour the mixture into small glasses or tea cups and chill.

When ready to serve, run a knife around the inside of the glasses and up-end the panna cotta onto a plate. Or, if you've used pretty tea cups, keep the panna cotta in the tea cups to serve. Decorate with violets.

Zucchini (Courgette) and pumpkin
Cucurbita pepo

GROWING: Zucchini are an annual compact vine with large hairy leaves and marrow-like fruit. Zucchini fruit may be green, striped or yellow depending upon the variety. Pumpkins have edible flowers and are also annuals. They are renowned as a boisterous vine that needs lots of space to grow. Both are cucurbits as they are in the family Cucurbitaceae.

To grow both, prepare the soil by adding a little lime or dolomite, manure or organic fertiliser. Sow 2 seeds per mound of soil about 30 cm x 30 cm and sow two seeds in the top of each mound. This allows good drainage and reduces the risk of root rot.

Male flowers of zucchini and pumpkins form on long stems. Female flowers form in front of the immature fruit. Once fertilised, the female flower drops off and the zucchini or pumpkin fruit continues to grow. Any type of zucchini or pumpkin flower can be eaten. Some zucchini, such as the Italian 'Le Bizarre' variety are bred for flower production rather than fruit size. They will produce copious numbers of flowers for you.

Cucurbits are prone to powdery mildew. Spray with seaweed solution to help strengthen the cell walls. If you see black and yellow ladybirds on the leaves, these are a sign that powdery mildew is not far away. Spray with organic potassium-based fungicides such as eco-fungicide.

HARVESTING AND EDIBLE PARTS: Harvest the male and female flowers on the morning they open. Remove the pollen bearing parts before use. I use a pair of tweezers or small scissors for this delicate task.

Fresh new leaf tips and stems are also edible.

COLOUR:	Yellow
SUN/SHADE:	Full sun
PLANTING:	Seed-after frost, spring to summer; in frost free areas-later winter to summer
FLOWERING:	50-65 days
HEIGHT:	Compact vines spread 1-2 m

Labna filled flowers on cauliflower pizza crust

This is a delicious pizza with a difference. The cauliflower in the base is an edible flower head too. It's a tasty option for those who are vegetarian or needing gluten free options. The crusts can be frozen for several weeks and the labna will need to be made in advance.

MAKES 2 PIZZAS GF, V

LABNA
2 cups natural full cream yoghurt
2 teaspoons rosemary, finely snipped
1 clove garlic, crushed
1 level teaspoon salt

CAULIFLOWER CRUST
½ large cauliflower (about 3 cups finely chopped)
¾ cup almonds, soaked 2 hours and drained
¼ cup chia seed
1 tablespoon psyllium husks
1 ½ tablespoons oregano, chopped
1 teaspoon cumin powder
salt and pepper

PIZZA TOPPING
½ cup sunflower and basil pesto from page 140
1 cup baby spinach leaves
8 artichoke hearts
8-10 basil leaves
½ red capsicum, sliced finely
salt and pepper to taste
12 zucchini or pumpkin flowers, stamens removed

TO SERVE: Nasturtium and viola flowers

LABNA: Blanch a piece of kitchen string and a piece of muslin or cheesecloth in boiling water to sterilise them. Sit a colander in a large bowl and line it with the muslin.

Add the yoghurt to a mixing bowl. Stir in the rosemary, garlic and salt until combined. Pour into the muslin. Gather the muslin in a bundle and tie with the string at the top. Leave the colander, bowl and bundle to drain in the fridge for 24-48 hours. Whey will drain into the bowl and the yoghurt will thicken to become labna. Use the whey in other recipes.

CAULIFLOWER CRUST: Heat the oven to 180°C. Add all the crust ingredients into a food processor. Process on medium speed until it becomes granular and begins to clump together. Divide the crust mixture into two portions. Press each portion into a 1cm thick circle on a baking paper lined tray. Cook for 25 minutes until golden around the edges.

Remove the crusts from the oven. Carefully spread ¼ cup pesto onto each pizza crust using the back of a tablespoon. Top with baby spinach, artichoke hearts, basil leaves and capsicum. Pipe labna into the zucchini flowers. Trim off the excess stems and lay five filled flowers onto each pizza. Add salt and pepper. Pop the pizzas under a grill to heat the toppings without burning.

Before serving, sprinkle over the extra flowers. The nasturtiums add a wonderful pepperiness to the pizza.

Rose petal and cornflower chai tea

When you make your own chai tea you'll be spoilt for flavour. This recipe is brim-full of rich flavours and colours.

GF, V, DF
4 cloves
1 cinnamon stick, crumbled
1 slice fresh ginger
1 vanilla bean
10 star anise
1 small strip of orange rind
5 cardamom pods, bruised
5 peppercorns, crushed
¼ cup dried rose petals
1 tablespoon dried cornflowers

Dry roast the spices in a frypan over medium heat until the fragrance rises. Remove from the heat and cool. Add rose petals and cornflowers.

Store the cooled chai spices in a jar. To brew, add 1 cup of water and 1 teaspoon of chai spices per person, to a saucepan. Simmer at least 5 minutes. Remove from heat and add green or black tea leaves, then serve.

Rose petal champagne sorbet

This is a romantic pink palate cleanser after a sumptuous high tea. It's also wonderful to indulge in on a hot day.

SERVES 8 GF, V, DF
100 g caster sugar
350 ml boiling water
Crushed petals of 3 fragrant red roses
1 teaspoon bottled rose water
60 ml lemon juice
200 ml champagne
2 bright red hibiscus flowers (optional)

TO SERVE: Crystallised flowers.

Combine sugar and boiling water in a bowl and stir to dissolve. Add the remaining ingredients, including the red hibiscus flowers (with stamens removed) if you have them. They add more colour to the sorbet. Set aside to cool. Strain out the flowers. Freeze, beating several times during the freezing process. Serve with crystallised flowers.

Lavender jelly

Lavender jelly stores well in the pantry. Refrigerate once opened. It is simply beautiful on scones, pikelets and with sponges and shortcakes.

GF, V, DF
1 kg granny smith apples
550 ml water
4 tablespoons lavender flowers
450 g white sugar, approximately
1 tablespoon white wine vinegar

Chop apples into rough pieces. Don't core or peel them. Add to a large saucepan with the water and lavender flowers. Simmer until very soft.

Line a colander with muslin or cheesecloth and sit it over a large bowl. Pour the apples and juice into the colander and drain all the juice. Tie the cloth with string and hang it over the bowl until it stops dripping. Don't squeeze the apples or your jelly will be cloudy.

Measure the juice into a large saucepan and add the vinegar plus 450 g sugar per 600 ml juice. Bring to the boil and simmer, until when tested, a teaspoonful of the jelly wrinkles when it cools on a saucer. It's now ready to seal into hot sterilised jars.

Floral butter

Butter flavoured and coloured with flowers is a tasty and beautiful addition to many simple foods. It is a favourite of ours when topping our own organic sweet corn cobs. The addition of herbs such as rosemary, thyme and lemon balm, add a fresh flavour to the butter.

GF, V
100 g softened butter
3 teaspoons dried or finely chopped fresh edible flower petals
1 teaspoon finely chopped herbs

Fold the petals and herbs into the butter. Dollop the pretty butter onto a sheet of baking paper and form into a log. Wrap in the paper and chill until needed.

When ready to use, slice off a chunky slice from the roll of butter. It adds colour and flavour to fresh vegies.

EDIBLE FLOWER SEED SOWING & FLOWERING			SOWING/PLANTING SEASON			
FLOWERS	TIME TO FLOWER	CULTIVATION MODE	TROPICAL	SUBTROPICAL	TEMPERATE	COOL, FROSTY
Banana Bell	Transplant to harvest: 11-14 months	suckers/tissue culture	All year	All year	Summer	X
Bean & pea	Seed to flower: 7-10 weeks	seed	All year	All year	All year	All year
Begonia	Cutting to flower: 12-24 weeks	cuttings	Autumn - spring	All year	Spring - autumn	Spring & summer -hot house
Blue Butterfly Vine	Seed to flower: 10-12 months	seed	Spring - summer	Spring - summer	Summer	X
Borage	Seed to flower: 12 weeks	seed	Spring - autumn	Spring - late summer	Autumn, spring	Spring - summer
Bougainvillea	Time to flower: 12-24 months	seed, cutting	Spring - autumn	Spring - autumn	Spring - autumn Frost free only	X
Calendula	Seed to flower: 10 weeks	seed	Mid summer- autumn, spring	Late summer- autumn, spring	Late summer- autumn, spring	Summer- autumn, spring
Chamomile	Seed to flower: 16 weeks	seed	Late winter, spring	Late winter - spring	Spring - summer	Spring- early summer
Chicory	Seed to flower	seed	Autumn, winter, spring	Autumn, winter, spring	Autumn, spring	Autumn, spring
Cornflower	Seed to flower: 14-20 weeks	seed	Autumn	Late summer- late autumn	Autumn - spring	Autumn, spring
Cosmos	Seed to flower: 12 weeks	seed	Winter, spring	Autumn, winter, spring	Spring , summer	Spring, summer
Crucifix Orchid	Keiki to flower: 12 months	Keiki	All year	Summer, autumn	Summer, autumn	As indoor plants only
Dahlia	Tuber to flower: 8 weeks	seed, tuber/rhizome	Spring	Spring	Spring	Spring-early summer
Daylily	Spring to summer after planting	seed, division	Any time	Any time	Any time	Spring, summer
Dianthus	Seed to flower: 20 weeks	seed, division	Autumn , winter, spring	Late summer, winter, spring	Late summer, winter, spring	Autumn, spring
Elderflower	Within 12 months	seed, cuttings, sucker	All year	All year	Spring, summer	Summer

These are a guide only. Planting & flowering times may vary within zones & plant species

EDIBLE FLOWER SEED SOWING & FLOWERING			SOWING/PLANTING SEASON			
FLOWERS	TIME TO FLOWER	CULTIVATION MODE	TROPICAL	SUBTROPICAL	TEMPERATE	COOL, FROSTY
Fennel	Seed to flower: 4-5 months	seed	Autumn-spring	All year	Winter, late spring, summer	Florence fennel only Tasmania. Spring to mid summer
Ginger-Galangal	Planting to flowering: 1-4 years	tuber/rhizome	After flowering	Late summer-winter	Hot spot only. Late summer	X
Ginger-Torch	Planting to flower: 1-2 years	tuber/rhizome	Autumn-winter	Spring, summer	Hot spot only. Late summer	X
Jasmine Sambac	Cuttings to flower: min. 12 months	cuttings	Autumn, winter	Spring, summer	Warm spot only. Spring, summer	X
Lavender	Up to 12 months	seed, cuttings	L. allardii in autumn, winter	Spring, early summer	Spring, early summer	Summer
Pumpkin	Seed to flower: 5-10 weeks	seed	Autumn, winter, spring (dry season)	Spring, early summer	Spring-early summer, autumn	Late spring to mid summer
Radish	Seed to flower: 6-8 weeks	seed	All year	All year	All year	Spring to early autumn
Rose	Cutting to flower: 4-12 months	cuttings	Mid winter, late summer	Mid winter, late summer	Autumn-spring	Autumn-spring
Rosella	Seed to flower: 12 weeks	seeds	Spring, summer	Spring, summer	Late spring, summer	X
Sesbiana	Seed to flower: 2 years	seeds	Winter, spring	Winter, spring	X	X
Snapdragon	Seed to flower: 16 weeks	seeds	Autumn-spring	Autumn, spring	Spring, summer	Late spring, summer
Society Garlic	Division to flower: 12-24 weeks	division	All year	All year	Late spring, summer	Early summer
Sunflower	Seed to flower 12 weeks	seed	All year	Late winter, spring-autumn	Spring -autumn	Spring, summer
Viola	Seed to flower 16 weeks	seed	Late summer, autumn	Late summer-early spring	Autumn-spring	Late summer, autumn, spring
Violets	Division to flower up to 12 months	division, seed	Native violet-cooler months	Divisions-spring, autumn. Seed autumn	Divisions all year. Seed autumn	Divisions all year. Seed autumn
Zucchini	Seed to flower 6-8 weeks	seed	All year	All year	Spring, summer	Late spring, summer

These are a guide only. Planting & flowering times may vary within zones & plant species

INDEX

RECIPES ARE INDICATED BY PAGE NUMBERS IN BOLD TYPE

Acknowledgements

To the amazingly supportive community of people who have helped me bring this book to life, I thank you. May your gardens flower abundantly!

My special thanks to Liam Brennan who gave countless hours and photographic expertise and to Damien, my husband, who provided patient and loving advice and proof reading. They are two terrific men in my life.

A friend and artist Jan Haughton brought the garden plans to life with her watercolours. And thanks to my daughters who added their language skills and journalistic expertise to the project.

Thanks to OCP (Organic Crop Protectants), Qld Organics and Green Harvest-companies who have supported my organic teaching for many years and who have also supported this book.

First published 2017 by Ecobotanica Pty Ltd., Capalaba Queensland
www.ecobotanica.com.au

Printed in China by the OPUS Group
National Library of Australia Catalogue-in-publication data are available
Linda Brennan, A Delicious Bunch-Growing and cooking with edible flowers

ISBN 978-0-646-97038-7

Disclaimer

The information in this book is designed to provide helpful information on growing, cooking and using edible flowers. This book is not meant to be used, nor should it be used, to diagnose or treat any medical condition. For diagnosis or treatment of any medical problem, consult your physician. The publisher and author are not responsible for any specific health or allergy consequences arising from the use of flowers referred to in this book. They are not liable for any damages or negative consequences from any recipe, treatment, action, application or preparation, to any person reading or following the information in this book.